# STUDIES

# IN MATHEMATICAL AND

# MANAGERIAL ECONOMICS

*Editor*

HENRI THEIL

VOLUME 9

1969

NORTH-HOLLAND PUBLISHING COMPANY
AMSTERDAM · LONDON

# THE EVALUATION OF RISKY INTERRELATED INVESTMENTS

*Budgeting Interrelated Activities – 1*

# THE EVALUATION
# OF RISKY INTERRELATED
# INVESTMENTS

*by*

## FREDERICK S. HILLIER

*Stanford University*

1969

NORTH-HOLLAND PUBLISHING COMPANY
AMSTERDAM · LONDON

Library of Congress Catalog Card Number: 79-97203
Standard Book Number: 7204 3309 6

PUBLISHERS:

NORTH-HOLLAND PUBLISHING COMPANY – AMSTERDAM
NORTH-HOLLAND PUBLISHING COMPANY, LTD. – LONDON

*This book is the first of two volumes on "Budgeting Interrelated Activities", prepared under the sponsorship of The Institute of Management Sciences (TIMS) and the Office of Naval Research (ONR), Washington, D.C.*

PRINTED IN THE NETHERLANDS

# INTRODUCTION TO THE SERIES

This is a series of books concerned with the quantitative approach to problems in the behavioural science field. The studies are in particular in the overlapping areas of mathematical economics, econometrics, operational research, and management science. Also, the mathematical and statistical techniques which belong to the apparatus of modern behavioural science have their place in this series. A well-balanced mixture of pure theory and practical applications is envisaged, which ought to be useful for universities and for research workers in business and government.

The Editor hopes that the volumes of this series, all of which relate to such a young and vigorous field of research activity, will contribute to the exchange of scientific information at a truly international level.

THE EDITOR

# PREFACE

The U.S. Office of Naval Research Monograph Series on Mathematical Methods in Logistics was initiated in 1963 with the publication of *Multistage Inventory Models and Techniques* (Stanford University Press) with H. E. Scarf, Dorothy M. Gilford and M. W. Shelly, editors. The second member of this series, "A Complete Constructive Algorithm for the General Mixed Linear Programming Problem", by Glenn W. Graves, was published in the Naval Research Logistics Quarterly 12, No. 1, March, 1965, pp. 1 ff. The present monograph is the first of two volumes which will constitute the third member of this series under the title of *Budgeting Interrelated Activities*.

The present volume, the first of this pair, is by Dr. Frederick S. Hillier of Stanford University's Department of Operations Research. It is an elaboration and extension of a paper submitted as part of an ONR (Office of Naval Research) and TIMS (The Institute of Management Sciences) sponsored program to encourage, or uncover, research in the area of "Capital Budgeting of Interrelated Projects". Dr. Hillier's paper was unanimously selected for the award by a committee, appointed by The Institute of Management Sciences, not only for their recognized competence and authority but also to reflect the international character of this part of the program. The members of this ONR-TIMS Awards Committee may be listed as follows:

Professor W. W. Cooper, Chairman of the
  the Committee
Dean, School of Urban and Public Affairs
Carnegie-Mellon University
Pittsburgh, Pennsylvania 15213

Dr. A. Charnes
The University of Texas System Professor
  and Jesse H. Jones Professor
The University of Texas System
Austin, Texas 78712

Dr. Jacques H. Dreze
Research Director, CORE
Université Catholique de Louvain
De Croylaan 54
Heverlee, Belgium

Professor T. Paulsson Frenckner
University of Stockholm
School of Economics
Sveavagen 65
Stockholm Va., Sweden

Professor Sigeiti Moriguti
Faculty of Engineering
University of Tokyo
Bunkyo-ku, Tokyo, Japan

Professor George Morton
Department of Economics
London School of Economics and Political
  Science
Houghton Street, Aldwych
London, W.C. 2, England

Dr. Henri Theil, Director
Center for Mathematical Studies in
  Business and Economics
The University of Chicago
Chicago, Illinois 60637

Dr. Harvey Wagner
Professor of Administrative Sciences
Yale University
New Haven, Connecticut

As in the previous cases, this committee functioned as part of a program designed to (1) encourage research in a relatively unexplored area of the management sciences and (2) identify new and promising talent for research which should be supported. In keeping with these objectives the committee judged all manuscripts in terms of (i) operational significance (ii) conceptual contribution or (iii) methodological development. For these purposes, operational significance was intended to refer to any potential for improved applications that a manuscript might suggest relative to the existing state of management budgetary practices. Conceptual contributions were deemed applicable when judging attempts to clarify, extend or unify budgetary constructs, or to relate them to constructs that might be found in investment or inventory analyses or other (possibly) related fields, especially when portfolio considerations or other types of interdependencies might be present or when short-term (operating) budgets and related schedules of production, employment, etc., might be identified with longer term (capital budgeting) considerations in an illuminating manner. Finally, methodological developments could be deemed to be present for evaluation in cases where manuscripts might contain suggestions for new management procedures (or institutions) as well as when new mathematics or computer codes, etc., were essayed.

An attempt was made to interpret these criteria in a very broad way, partly because it was recognized that research activity in this area has been (and continues to be) fairly light and partly because one objective of the contest was to uncover new research talent. Although any one of these sets of criteria could have been used as a basis for the award, no such exclusive choice between these three sets was necessary. The manuscript submitted by Professor Hillier has very high potential in all three areas – conceptual, methodological and operational – as will be apparent, we think, to all who study its elaboration in the present volume. Perhaps even more important, however, is the fact that the completion and publication of this part of Dr. Hillier's research will also provide a basis from which to extend the present state of managerial-scientific knowledge and practice by further research in this area – a main objective of the ONR-TIMS program.

It should perhaps be said that one part of the award to Dr. Hillier consisted of a research grant from the U.S. Office of Naval Research under which he was enabled to secure time and support for extending the research and perfecting the manuscript which he had originally submitted to the ONR-TIMS Committee. After this award was made, the undersigned editorial committee was then appointed (a) to assist Dr. Hillier by reviewing his manuscript in detail as well as (b) to assemble additional manuscripts for publication in a volume on "Capital Budgeting of Interrelated Projects". Ensuing developments, however, made it desirable to alter the plan which had originally been proposed for the editorial committee. First, the scarcity of research in the contest area plus the existence of significant research in other areas of budgeting made it desirable to augment the scope of the publication and to alter its title to the present one – viz., *Budgeting Interrelated Activities*. Second, the extension and further developments from the additional research undertaken by Dr. Hillier, after the contest had terminated, made it desirable to publish his own contribution in the separate volume which appears in the pages that follow. Thus the reader's attention is now invited to

Frederick S. Hillier's *The Evaluation of Risky Interrelated Investments* as a distinguished contribution to an important, but difficult, and neglected, area of work. We hope that its companion will soon be forthcoming as *Studies in Budgeting*, the second of these two volumes of research which will result from this ONR-TIMS program to supply new approaches and insight into a relatively neglected area of work.

Acknowledgments are due to many people, but we would particularly like to single out (1) Dr. Maynard W. Shelly, formerly of the U.S. Office of Naval Research, and now at the University of Kansas, and (2) Dr. Robert M. Thrall of Rice University, for their imaginative help and guidance on all parts of the programs and related developments that have led to the development of the U.S. Office of Naval Research Monograph Series on Mathematical Methods in Logistics.

R. F. BYRNE
A. CHARNES
W. W. COOPER
O. DAVIS
DOROTHY GILFORD

# TABLE OF CONTENTS

# CHAPTER 1

# INTRODUCTION

## 1.1. General description of the problem

The amount of risk involved is often one of the important considerations in the evaluation of proposed investments. This is especially true when the investments are sufficiently large that the failure to achieve expectations could significantly affect the financial position of the individual or firm. A recent paper by this writer (HILLIER 1963) has explored the problem of evaluating a single risky investment or a set of independent risky investments. However, the desirability of one prospective investment is not always a question that can be answered independently of others, since their performances often would be interrelated. These interrelationships may take on many different forms. Some investments may be competitive, such as developing new products which would, in part, compete for the same market. Some investments may be complementary, such as developing and installing new production systems which would share common facilities or which would mutually benefit from common research and development work. The amount of income resulting from each of a group of investments may be correlated because these incomes are affected by common factors. These factors may be internal to the firm or they may be exogenous factors, such as the general state of the economy or relevant technological advances.

Interrelationships between investments directly affect the total risk involved in making these investments. Therefore, a truly satisfactory investment decision would give full consideration to these interrelationships and to the consequent risks involved. The objective of this book is to initiate explorations on developing systematic procedures for evaluating a set of large, risky, interrelated investments.

## 1.2. Previous relevant work

Previous proposals for dealing with risk have been summarized elsewhere (HILLIER 1963). However, for the sake of completeness, directly related previous work will be mentioned again.

A general framework for evaluating risky investments was developed by LUTZ and LUTZ in 1951. Much of this and related work was then synthesized by FARRAR (1962) in the process of developing and testing a particular investment decision model. MASSÉ (1962) also has given a rigorous survey of work done by him and others in this area.

MARKOWITZ (1959) has very thoroughly and competently treated one special case of the general problem of evaluating risky, interrelated investments, namely, the analysis of portfolios containing large numbers of securities. Markowitz begins by formulating a static model of the problem which is an assumed deterministic equivalent of some model under risk or uncertainty. Given this formulation, he then shows how to determine the portfolio which provides the most suitable combination of expected rate of return and standard deviation of rate of return. This research has subsequently motivated related work by CHENG (1962), SHARPE (1963), BAUMOL (1963), FAMA (1965), and MAO and SÄRNDAL (1966). NASLUND and WHINSTON (1962) have developed a different (mathematical programming) approach to this problem of investment in the stock market.

WEINGARTNER (1963) has comprehensively applied linear programming and integer programming to various problems of capital budgeting under certainty, especially investment planning under capital rationing and under imperfect capital markets. Much of this work was built upon earlier research by CHARNES and COOPER (1961, 1962a), and especially by CHARNES et al. (1959).

The reader is referred to the bibliography, and to a survey paper on evaluating interrelated investments by WEINGARTNER (1966), for relevant work done by other scholars too numerous to mention here.

While the above work and, to a lesser extent, other research listed in the bibliography have suggested a few relevant ideas, this paper is largely the result of greatly extending and generalizing the elementary ideas presented in an earlier paper by this writer (HILLIER 1963). The problem considered in this paper is that of evaluating a risky investment which would generate one or more mutually independent series of normally distributed cash flows, where the cash flows within each series are either mutually independent or perfectly correlated. The probability distribution of present value (and of other measures) was then obtained. The paper then described how to obtain the probability distribution of present value (and of other measures) and suggested how this information might be used in the decision process. This type of approach has since been discussed further by HERTZ (1964), HILLIER (1965), HILLIER and HEEBINK (1965–66), and HOROWITZ (1966), and has been extended to a decision tree format by HESPOS and STRASSMANN (1965).

## 1.3. The present value criterion

There now appears to be a substantial weight of opinion among economists and related academicians that the present value criterion is usually the most appropriate one for evaluating investments. This is the criterion that will be used here.

For purposes of defining present value, consider an investment or set of investments which may generate incoming (positive) or outgoing (negative) cash flows (including imputed cash flows) immediately and during some or all of the next $n$ time periods, but not thereafter.[1] Let $X_j$ be the random variable which takes on the value of the net cash flow during time period $j$, where $j = 0, 1, 2, ..., n$. Let $i_j$ be the rate of interest, commonly referred to as the cost of capital, which properly reflects the investor's time value and time preference of money during time period $j$. The present value, $P$, of this investment or set of investments can then be

---

[1] Therefore, $n = \infty$ in principle if cash flows would be generated perpetually. Section A.3 discusses practical considerations in the selection of $n$.

defined as

$$P = \sum_{j=0}^{n} \left[ \frac{X_j}{\prod\limits_{k=1}^{j} (1+i_k)} \right].$$

The common practice in using the present value criterion is to treat $X_j (j=0, 1, ..., n)$ and therefore $P$ as if they were constants. This procedure essentially amounts to estimating $E(X_j)$, $(j=0, 1, ..., n)$, and then computing $E(P)$ to find "the" present value. The objective is to select the combination of investments which maximizes $E(P)$.

The model used in this book will explicitly recognize that $P$ is usually a random variable. It will then explicitly consider the risk involved in making any set of investments by examining the pattern of variation of $X_j (j=0, 1, ..., n)$, and therefore of $P$, from their expectations. The solution procedure will then select the combination of investments which, in effect, has the most favorable probability distribution of $P$.

## 1.4. The expected utility criterion

Even if one succeeds in obtaining the probability distribution of $P$ for each feasible combination of investments, the selection of the "best" combination, i.e., the one yielding the most favorable distribution, may not be obvious. A systematic procedure for making this selection, e.g., a selection procedure which may be carried out on an electronic computer, requires an additional single-valued criterion which summarizes the information provided by the distribution of $P$. Such a criterion will be obtained by means of an utilitarian approach.

In a monumental work, VON NEUMANN and MORGENSTERN (1953) developed the essence of modern utility theory (and game theory). Very roughly, their assumptions essentially are that the decision maker can

(1) give a consistent preference order for all alternatives or events of interest, and

(2) express consistent preferences for combinations of events and stated probabilities.

Under these assumptions, Von Neumann and Morgenstern show that one can introduce utility associations to the basic alternatives in such a manner that, if the decision maker is guided solely by the expected utility, he is acting in accord with his true tastes.[1]

The subsequent formulation in this paper assumes that the Von Neumann–Morgenstern requirements hold so that expected utility is the appropriate criterion. It is further assumed that the only alternative outcomes or events of interest are the alternative values of the present value generated by the approved set of investments. In other words, it is assumed that utility is a function[2] only of present value and is therefore independent of the identity of the investments or the pattern of cash flows which yield the present value.[3] This reduces the problem to determining the feasible set of investments whose probability distribution of present value maximizes expected utility.[4]

### 1.5. Feasibility considerations

It may not be feasible to approve all subsets of the set of proposed investments. For example, budget constraints may restrict the investment possibilities. Some investments are mutually exclusive, such as when they involve different methods for providing the same service, so that no more than one of these investments can be approved. The set may include contingent investments whose approval is dependent on the approval of one or more other investments. Limitations on required resources such

---

[1] The reader is referred also to LUCE and RAIFFA (1957, Chapter 2) for a precise statement of the assumptions and conclusion.

[2] The Von Neumann–Morgenstern procedure determines a utility function which is unique only up to a linear transformation. In order to uniquely specify the utility function, the convention will be adopted here that the function goes through the origin with slope one.

[3] This assumption will be relaxed in Chapter 7.

[4] See Section 4.3 for a brief discussion of the case where the utility function cannot be determined.

as labor and materials may rule out certain combinations of projects.[1]

It is clear that any systematic procedure for selecting the best set of investments must take such feasibility constraints into account.

## 1.6. Statement of problem

Consider a set of $m$ proposed investments. Define the decision variable $\delta_k$ as

$$\delta_k = \begin{cases} 1, \text{ if the } k\text{th proposed investment is approved}, \\ \\ 0, \text{ if the } k\text{th proposed investment is rejected}, \end{cases}$$

for $k = 1, 2, ..., m$. No decisions other than approval and rejection will be considered. However, it should be emphasized that "investment" here may be defined in a broad sense so as to include investment strategies and combinations of investments. Thus, other decisions such as "postpone the investment for a year" or "try a pilot run first" may be taken into account by treating the alternatives as mutually exclusive investments to be approved or rejected. Similarly, alternative strategies, such as "try project A for a year and then switch to project B if the losses are more than $x$ dollars" for several different values of $x$, may also be treated as mutually exclusive investments which may be contingent upon certain other decisions (such as not undertaking project B immediately).[2] Furthermore, if certain investments are so highly interrelated that it may be difficult to analyze their interactions, then it may be more convenient to consider the various feasible combinations of these investments as single "derived" investments that are mutually exclusive.

Let $\boldsymbol{\delta} = (\delta_1, \delta_2, ..., \delta_m)$. Assume that the investments may generate incoming (positive) or outgoing (negative) cash flows immediately and

---

[1] WEINGARTNER (1963, Sections 2.3, 3.6, 3.7, 7.1, 7.2, etc.) discusses these and other constraints and how to express them mathematically in a linear programming formulation.
[2] A more direct method of making such "second-stage decisions" also will be introduced in Chapter 7.

during some or all of the next $n$ time periods, but not thereafter. Let the random variable $X_j(\delta)$ be the net cash flow during time period $j$ ($j = 0, 1, ..., n$) resulting from the decision $\delta$. Let $i_j(\delta)$ be the cost of capital, given $\delta$, during time period $j$ ($j = 1, 2, ..., n$).[1] Let $U(p)$ be the utility if $p$ is the realized present value of the approved set of investments. Let $S$ be the set of feasible solutions, i.e., the subset of $\{\delta|\ \delta_k = 0 \text{ or } 1\ ; k = 1, 2, ..., m\}$ whose elements are feasible decision vectors.

The problem that will be considered in Chapters 2–6 is to determine $\delta \in S$ so as to

$$\text{Maximize } E\{U(P(\delta))\}\ , \text{ where}$$
$$\qquad\quad {\scriptstyle \delta \in S}$$

$$P(\delta) = \sum_{j=0}^{n} \frac{X_j(\delta)}{\displaystyle\sum_{k=1}^{j}\ (1 + i_k(\delta))} .$$

This problem will be reformulated in a chance-constrained programming format in Chapter 7.


## 1.7. Overview

If one could find $E\{U(P(\delta))\}$ for each $\delta \in S$, the optimal $\delta$ could then be obtained by exhaustive enumeration. Chapter 2 derives conditions which the optimal $\delta$ must satisfy, thereby suggesting more efficient solution procedures.

Chapter 3 develops one particular model for describing a proposed set of risky interrelated investments. This model is intended to facilitate determining the mean and variance of present value $P(\delta)$.

Chapter 4 discusses the probability distribution of $P(\delta)$. The bulk of the discussion concerns conditions under which this distribution would be approximately normal.

---

[1] It is assumed throughout this book that $i_j(\delta)$ is known. However, the precise determination of its proper value is a deep theoretical question which continues to receive serious study elsewhere. In practice, it is common to estimate only one value $i$ which is then used for all time periods and decisions.

Chapter 5 deals with finding expected utility. Several models for utility functions are developed, and solutions or approximate solutions for the expected utility are obtained under various conditions.

Chapter 6 then draws upon the preceding chapters in order to develop systematic solution procedures. Both an approximate linear programming approach and an exact branch-and-bound algorithm are presented.

Chapter 7 enlarges the problem to include the impact of other factors over time. A chance-constrained programming approach is formulated, and both exact and approximate solution procedures are described.

The Appendix makes numerous suggestions regarding practical implementation.

# CHAPTER 2

# NECESSARY CONDITIONS FOR OPTIMALITY

Since $S$ is a finite set, it is evident that, in principle, one could find the optimal $\delta$ by exhaustive enumeration, given that $E\{U(P(\delta))\}$ can be computed for each $\delta \in S$. However, since the number of elements in $S$ may be as large as $2^m$, the computation time required may be prohibitively large even for today's elelctronic computers, when $m$ is fairly large. Therefore, it would be very helpful if more efficient solution procedures could be developed. Furthermore, additional information on the characteristics of the optimal $\delta$ would be useful and enlightening. The objective of this chapter will be to derive such information and thereby permit eliminating many or most of the $\delta$ vectors from consideration without calculating $E\{U(P(\delta))\}$. This will expedite finding the optimal $\delta$ by either exhaustive enumeration or the branch-and-bound algorithm described in Chapter 6.

A condition imposed on most of the results of this chapter is that the utility function, $U(p)$, is a monotonic increasing concave function, which implies that $U'(p) \geqslant 0$ and $U''(p) \leqslant 0$ for all $p$ at which $U(p)$ is twice differentiable. This condition merely describes the usual situation where increasing the present value from $p$ to $p+\varepsilon$, $\varepsilon > 0$, would be considered desirable but would yield no greater increment to utility when $p$ is large than when $p$ is small. This is consistent with the economist's traditional hypothesis of decreasing marginal utility.

Another condition imposed on some of the subsequent results is that $P(\delta)$ has a symmetrical probability distribution, i.e., a distribution whose probability density function is symmetrical about the mean. One distribution with this property is, of course, the normal distribution. Section 4.2 will discuss the conditions under which $P(\delta)$ is normal.

**Definition:** Two random variables, say $W_1$ and $W_2$, will be said to have distributions with the *same functional form* if $\dfrac{W_1 - E(W_1)}{\sqrt{\text{Var}(W_1)}}$ and $\dfrac{W_2 - E(W_2)}{\sqrt{\text{Var}(W_1)}}$ are identically distributed.

**Lemma 1:** Let $g(w)$ be a concave function. Let $W_1$ and $W_2$ be random variables which have symmetrical distributions with the same functional forms, both with mean zero, and with variance $\sigma_1^2$ and $\sigma_2^2$, respectively. If $\sigma_2^2 \geqslant \sigma_1^2$, then $E\{g(W_2)\} \leqslant E\{g(W_1)\}$.

**Proof:** Assume that $\sigma_2^2 \geqslant \sigma_1^2$, and set $k = \dfrac{\sigma_2}{\sigma_1}$. Thus, $k \geqslant 1$. Let $f_1(w)$ and $f_2(w)$ be the probability density functions for $W_1$ and $W_2$, respectively. By concavity,

$$\tfrac{1}{2}[g(kw) + g(-kw)] \leqslant \tfrac{1}{2}[g(w) + g(-w)],$$

since $k \geqslant 1$, so that

$$g(kw) - g(w) \leqslant g(-w) - g(-kw).$$

Therefore, if $f_1(w)$ is a continuous function, then

$$E\{g(W_2)\} - E\{g(W_1)\} = \int_{-\infty}^{\infty} [g(w)f_2(w) - g(w)f_1(w)]\,dw$$

$$= \int_{-\infty}^{\infty} [g(kw) - g(w)]f_1(w)\,dw$$

$$= \int_{0}^{\infty} [(g(kw) - g(w)) - (g(-w) - g(-kw))]f_1(w)\,dw$$

$$\leqslant 0.$$

If $f_1(w)$ is not continuous, then using Riemann–Stieltjes integration yields the same result, which completes the proof.

**Theorem 1:** Assume that $U(p)$ is a monotonic increasing concave function. Consider $\delta^{(1)} \in S$ and $\delta^{(2)} \in S$. Assume that $P(\delta^{(1)})$ and $P(\delta^{(2)})$ have symmetrical distributions with the same functional form. Denote the mean and variance of $P(\delta^{(1)})$ and of $P(\delta^{(2)})$ by $\mu_1, \sigma_1^2$ and $\mu_2, \sigma_2^2$, respectively. If $\mu_1 \geqslant \mu_2$ and $\sigma_1^2 \leqslant \sigma_2^2$, then $E\{U(P(\delta^{(1)}))\} \geqslant E\{U(P(\delta^{(2)}))\}$.

**Proof:** Assume that the theorem is true in general for $\mu_1 = \mu_2$. Then it must be true for $\mu_1 > \mu_2$ for the following obvious reasons. Assume $\mu_1 - \mu_2 = \varepsilon > 0$. Define $P_2' \equiv P(\delta^{(2)}) + \varepsilon$. Since $E\{P_2'\} = \mu_1$, $E\{U(P(\delta^{(1)}))\} \geqslant E\{U(P_2')\}$ by assumption. Letting $f(p)$ be the density function for $P(\delta^{(2)})$,

$$E\{U(P(\delta^{(2)}))\} - E\{U(P_2')\} = \int_{-\infty}^{\infty} [U(p) - U(p+\varepsilon)]f(p)\,dp \leqslant 0,$$

since $U(p) \leqslant U(p+\varepsilon)$ because $U(p)$ is a monotonic increasing function.

Therefore, it is sufficient to prove the theorem for $\mu_1 = \mu_2$. Denote this common mean by $\mu$. Let $f_1(p)$ and $f_2(p)$ be the probability density functions for $P(\delta^{(1)})$ and $P(\delta^{(2)})$, respectively. Let $f_3(p)$ and $f_4(p)$ be probability density functions which are identical to $f_1(p)$ and $f_2(p)$, respectively, except that their means are translated down to zero. Then, if $\sigma_1^2 \leqslant \sigma_2^2$, it follows that

$$E\{U(P(\delta^{(2)}))\} = \int_{-\infty}^{\infty} U(p)f_2(p)\,dp$$

$$= \int_{-\infty}^{\infty} U(p+\mu)f_4(p)\,dp$$

$$\leqslant \int_{-\infty}^{\infty} U(p+\mu)f_3(p)\,dp$$

$$= E\{U(P(\delta^{(1)}))\}$$

by Lemma 1, which completes the proof.

**Corollary 1:** Assume that $U(p)$ is a monotonic increasing concave function. Let $P$ be a symmetrical random variable with mean $\mu$ and variance $\sigma^2$. Then, with $\mu$ fixed, $E\{U(P)\}$ is a monotonic decreasing function of $\sigma^2$. With $\sigma^2$ fixed, $E\{U(P)\}$ is a monotonic increasing function of $\mu$.

**Corollary 2:** Assume that $U(P)$ is a monotonic increasing concave function and that $P(\delta)$ has a symmetrical distribution with the same functional form for all $\delta \in S$. Consider any $\delta' \in S$ and let $T = \{\delta | \delta \in S$ and $\delta_k \leqslant \delta'_k$ for all $k = 1, ..., m\} - \{\delta'\}$, so that $\delta'$ can be obtained from any $\delta \in T$ by changing certain components of $\delta$ from zero to one. Then $\delta'$ is not an optimal solution (or at least not a unique one) if $E\{P(\delta')\} \leqslant E\{P(\delta)\}$ and $\text{Var}\{P(\delta')\} \geqslant \text{Var}\{P(\delta)\}$ for any $\delta \in T$.

**Corollary 3:** Assume that $U(p)$ is a monotonic increasing concave function. Consider a sequence of feasible $\delta$ vectors, $\{\delta^{(1)}, \delta^{(2)}, ..., \delta^{(N)}\}$, such that $E\{P(\delta^{(1)})\} \geqslant E\{P(\delta^{(2)})\} \geqslant ... \geqslant E\{P(\delta^{(N)})\}$. Assume that $P(\delta^{(j)})$ has a symmetrical distribution with the same functional form for $j = 1, 2, ..., N$. Then $\delta^{(j)}$ is not an optimal solution (or at least not a unique one) if there exists a positive integer $k$, $k < j$, such that $\text{Var}\{P(\delta^{(k)})\} \leqslant \text{Var}\{P(\delta^{(j)})\}$.

Theorem 1 and its corollaries should considerably reduce the number of $\delta$ vectors for which $E\{U(P(\delta))\}$ need be calculated for the usual case where $U(p)$ is a monotonic increasing concave function. Corollary 2 indicates that one can immediately reject any investment or combination of investments whose incremental contribution to expected present value is always negative, provided that its approval could not decrease the variance of total present value. Corollary 3 suggests that one should attempt to begin by considering the $\delta$ which maximizes $E\{P(\delta)\}$ and then consider remaining $\delta$ vectors in the order (more or less) of decreasing $E\{P(\delta)\}$ values. Using this procedure, one would maintain a record of the minimum $\text{Var}\{P(\delta)\}$ value considered thus far, and ignore any new $\delta$ vectors whose variance exceeds this minimum. Whenever it is inconvenient to examine the $\delta$ vectors in strictly this order, one can maintain a record of the minimum $\text{Var}\{P(\delta)\}$ value over each of a number of ranges of values of $E\{P(\delta)\}$.

Theorem 1 suggested how to identify some of the non-optimal $\delta$ vectors by comparing the probability distributions of $P(\delta)$ for all $\delta \in S$. However, two of the assumptions imposed may be fairly restrictive, viz., $P(\delta)$ has a symmetrical distribution and $U(p)$ is a concave function. The next theorem gives a corresponding result which does not require either of these assumptions.

**Theorem 2:** Assume that $U(p)$ is a monotonic increasing function. Consider $\delta^{(1)} \in S$ and $\delta^{(2)} \in S$. Assume that $U(P(\delta^{(1)}))$ and $U(P(\delta^{(2)}))$ have finite variances. If $P(\delta^{(1)})$ is stochastically larger than $P(\delta^{(2)})$, i.e., if $\text{Prob}\{P(\delta^{(1)}) > p\} \geqslant \text{Prob}\{P(\delta^{(2)}) > p\}$ for all $p$, then $E\{U(P(\delta^{(1)}))\} \geqslant E\{U(P(\delta^{(2)}))\}$.

**Proof:** Define $F_i(x) = \text{Prob}\{U(P(\delta^{(i)})) \leqslant x\}$ for $i = 1, 2$. Since $U(p)$ is monotonic increasing,

$$F_i(x) = \sup_{\{p:U(p) \leqslant x\}} \text{Prob}\{P(\delta^{(i)}) \leqslant p\} .$$

Therefore, assuming that $P(\delta^{(1)})$ is stochastically larger than $P(\delta^{(2)})$ implies that $U(P(\delta^{(1)}))$ is stochastically larger than $U(P(\delta^{(2)}))$, so that $F_1(x) \leqslant F_2(x)$ for all $x$.

$$E\{U(P(\delta^{(i)}))\} = \int_{-\infty}^{\infty} x\, dF_i(x) = \lim_{t \to \infty} \int_{-t}^{t} x\, dF_i(x) .$$

Using integration by parts,

$$\int_{-t}^{t} x\, dF_i(x) = t(F_i(t) + F_i(-t)) + \int_{-t}^{t} F_i(x)\, dx$$

$$= tF_i(-t) - t(1 - F_i(t)) + \int_0^t [1 - F_i(x)]\, dx - \int_{-t}^0 F_i(x)\, dx .$$

Since $U(P(\delta^{(i)}))$ has a finite variance, it is readily verified that

$$\lim_{t \to \infty} tF_i(-t) = 0 \quad \text{and} \quad \lim_{t \to \infty} t(1 - F_i(t)) = 0 .$$

Therefore,

$$E\{U(P(\delta^{(i)}))\} = \int_0^{\infty} [1 - F_i(x)]\, dx - \int_{-\infty}^0 F_i(x)\, dx .$$

Since $F_1(x) \leqslant F_2(x)$ for all $x$ under the hypothesis, it now follows that

$$E\{U(P(\delta^{(1)}))\} \geqslant E\{U(P(\delta^{(2)}))\} ,$$

which is the desired result.

Theorem 2 indicates that one may ignore any $\delta$ vector whose cumulative distribution function of present value is uniformly larger than that for some other $\delta \in S$.

One undesirable feature of the procedure suggested by the above results is that it does not stop until the $\delta$ vectors are exhausted. The optimal $\delta$ vector usually would involve approving most of the investments not vetoed by Corollary 2, and it therefore would be considered relatively early in the process. But the procedure requires going on to consider the huge number of uninteresting combinations where many of the investments not vetoed by Corollary 2 are still rejected, and therefore both the means and variances of total present value are much lower. The following theorems rectify this by establishing a lower bound on $E\{P(\delta)\}$, below which $\delta$ need not be considered.

**Theorem 3:** Assume that $U(p)$ is a concave function. Then $E\{U(P(\delta))\} \leqslant U(E\{P(\delta)\}) \leqslant E\{P(\delta)\}.$[1]

**Proof:** Section 1.4 imposed the restriction on $U(p)$ that $U(0) = 0$ and $U'(0) = 1$. This restriction and the assumption that $U(p)$ is a concave function implies that $U(p) \leqslant p$ for all $p$. Therefore, $U(E\{P(\delta)\}) \leqslant E\{P(\delta)\}$, and the second inequality is verified.

Denote $U^*(p) = U(E\{P(\delta)\}) + [p - E\{P(\delta)\}]U'(E\{P(\delta)\})$. Since $U(p)$ is a concave function, $U(p) \leqslant U^*(p)$ for all $p$. Therefore, $E\{U(P(\delta))\} \leqslant E\{U^*(P(\delta))\}$. But the definition of $U^*(p)$ implies that $E\{U^*(P(\delta))\} = U(E\{P(\delta)\})$. These last two results imply the first inequality of the theorem.

**Corollary 1:** Assume that $U(p)$ is a concave function. Consider $\delta^{(1)} \in S$ and $\delta^{(2)} \in S$. If $U(E\{P(\delta^{(2)})\}) \leqslant E\{U(P(\delta^{(1)}))\}$, then $E\{U(P(\delta^{(2)}))\} \leqslant E\{U(P(\delta^{(1)}))\}$.

**Corollary 2:** Assume that $U(p)$ is a monotonic increasing concave function. Consider a set $S_1 \subset S$ and define $S_2 = S - S_1$. Suppose that $\delta^*$ maximizes $E\{U(P(\delta))\}$ from among $\delta \in S_1$. Define $p^*$ by the equation,

---

[1] The first inequality has also been obtained in a mathematical programming context by Madansky and others.

$U(p^*) = E\{U(P(\delta^*))\}.$ [1] Then $\delta \in S_2$ is not an optimal solution (or at least not a unique one) if $E\{P(\delta)\} \leqslant p^*$.

**Proof:** Since $U(p)$ is a monotonic increasing function, $E\{P(\delta)\} \leqslant p^*$ implies that $U(E\{P(\delta)\}) \leqslant U(p^*)$. Since $U(p^*) = E\{U(P(\delta^*))\}$, the desired result now follows directly from Corollary 1.

A useful interpretation of Corollary 2 is that $S_1$ is the set of $\delta$ vectors already investigated so that $\delta^*$ is the best $\delta$ vector found so far. Any new $\delta$ vector (i.e., any element of $S_2$) can be eliminated from consideration immediately in favor of $\delta^*$ if $E\{P(\delta)\} \leqslant p^*$. Otherwise, it may be necessary to compute $E\{U(P(\delta))\}$ and compare it with $E\{U(P(\delta^*))\}$ to determine which element of $S$ is the best thus far considered.

**Lemma 2:** Let $P_1$ and $P_2$ be random variables with symmetrical distributions which are identical except for their means, which are $\mu_1$ and $\mu_2$, respectively, where $\mu_1 \leqslant \mu_2$. Assume that $U(p + \mu_2 - \mu_1) - U(p) \geqslant \varepsilon(\mu_2 - \mu_1)$ for all $p$. Then $E\{U(P_1)\} + \varepsilon(\mu_2 - \mu_1) \leqslant E\{U(P_2)\}$.

**Proof:** Let $f_1(p)$ be the probability density function of $P_1$. Then

$$E\{U(P_2)\} - E\{U(P_1)\} = \int_{-\infty}^{\infty} [U(p + (\mu_2 - \mu_1)) - U(p)] f_1(p) dp$$
$$\geqslant \varepsilon(\mu_2 - \mu_1),$$

since $U(p + (\mu_2 - \mu_1)) - U(p) \geqslant \varepsilon(\mu_2 - \mu_1)$ for all $p$.

**Theorem 4:** Assume that $U(p)$ is a concave function and that $U(p + x) - U(p) \geqslant \varepsilon x > 0$ for all $p$ and $x > 0$.[2] Consider two disjoint subsets of $S$, call them $S_1$ and $S_2$. Suppose that $\delta^*$ maximizes $E\{U(P(\delta))\}$ from among $\delta \in S_1$. Assume that the distribution of $P(\delta^*)$ and of $P(\delta)$ are symmetrical and have the same functional form for all $\delta \in S_2$. Define $\sigma_{min}^2 = \min_{\delta \in S_2}$

---

[1] The value $p^*$ must exist by the intermediate value theorem for continuous functions; $U(p)$ is necessarily continuous since it is concave (see EGGLESTON 1958, p. 46).
[2] If the derivative $U'(p)$ exists everywhere, the latter condition is implied if $\lim_{p \to \infty} U'(p) \geqslant \varepsilon > 0$, since $U(p)$ is concave.

$\text{Var}\{P(\delta)\}$. Suppose that $\sigma^2_{\min} < \text{Var}\{P(\delta^*)\}$. Let $P^*$ be the random variable whose distribution has the same functional form and mean as the distribution of $P(\delta^*)$ but whose variance is $\sigma^2_{\min}$. Then $\delta \in S_2$ is not an optimal solution (or at least not a unique one) if

$$E\{P(\delta)\} \leqslant E\{P(\delta^*)\} - \frac{E\{U(P^*)\} - E\{U(P(\delta^*))\}}{\varepsilon}.$$

**Proof:** Assume that $\delta \in S_2$ and

$$E\{P(\delta)\} \leqslant E\{P(\delta^*)\} - \frac{E\{U(P^*)\} - E\{U(P(\delta^*))\}}{\varepsilon}.$$

Corollary 1 to Theorem 1 implies that

$$E\{U(P(\delta^*))\} \leqslant E\{U(P^*)\}.$$

Let $P_1$ be the random variable whose distribution has the same functional form and mean as the distribution of $P(\delta)$ but whose variance is $\sigma^2_{\min}$. Hence, $E\{U(P(\delta))\} \leqslant E\{U(P_1)\}$ by Corollary 1 to Theorem 1. Therefore, since $E\{P_1\} = E\{P(\delta)\} \leqslant E\{P(\delta^*)\} = E\{P^*\}$, Lemma 2 yields

$$E\{U(P^*)\} \geqslant E\{U(P_1)\} + \varepsilon(E\{P^*\} - E\{P_1\})$$
$$\geqslant E\{U(P(\delta))\} + \varepsilon(E\{P(\delta^*)\} - E\{P(\delta)\}).$$

Rewriting the assumed inequality at the beginning of the proof,

$$\varepsilon(E\{P(\delta^*)\} - E\{P(\delta)\}) \geqslant E\{U(P^*)\} - E\{U(P(\delta^*))\}.$$

Combining these last two results gives

$$E\{U(P^*)\} \geqslant E\{U(P(\delta))\} + E\{U(P^*)\} - E\{U(P(\delta^*))\}.$$

Canceling common terms and rewriting,

$$E\{U(P(\delta^*))\} \geqslant E\{U(P(\delta))\},$$

which implies that $\delta$ is not a (unique) optimal solution, as was to be shown.

One useful interpretation of Theorem 4 is similar to that for Corollary 2 to Theorem 3. This interpretation is that $S_1$ is the set of $\delta$ vectors already investigated so that $\delta^*$ is the best $\delta$ vector found so far. $S_2$ is any convenient subset of the $\delta$ vectors remaining to be investigated. Any $\delta \in S_2$ can be eliminated from consideration immediately if the indicated inequality holds. Thus, Theorem 4 can be used to establish a lower bound on admissible values of $E\{P(\delta)\}$ over a certain class of $\delta$ vectors, e.g., those $\delta$ vectors such that $\Sigma_{k=1}^{m} \delta_k$ is some fixed constant. This would be useful when this lower bound is larger than the lower bound provided by Corollary 2 to Theorem 3.

To summarize, some of the applied results in this chapter assume that $U(p)$ is a monotonic increasing concave function and that $P(\delta)$ has a symmetrical distribution. Corollary 2 to Theorem 1 enables one to immediately reject certain investments. Corollary 3 to Theorem 1 permits rejecting all $\delta$ vectors such that there exists another feasible $\delta$ vector whose present value has both a larger mean and a smaller variance. Theorem 2 allows rejecting any $\delta$ vector whose cumulative distribution function of present value is uniformly larger than that for another feasible $\delta$ vector. Corollary 2 to Theorem 3 and Theorem 4 provide lower bounds on $E\{P(\delta)\}$, below which $\delta$ can be rejected. The problem could then be solved by calculating $E\{U(P(\delta))\}$ for all remaining feasible $\delta$ vectors, and selecting that $\delta$ which maximizes $E\{U(P(\delta))\}$. Alternative solution procedures that may be more efficient when $m$ is large will be presented in Chapter 6.

# CHAPTER 3

# A MODEL OF CASH FLOWS

The motivation for this chapter is expressed in the following thought. "Somewhere between the specific that has no meaning and the general that has no content there must be, for each purpose and at each level of abstraction, an optimum degree of generality."[1] Thus far, the problem has been considered only in terms of the total net cash flow, $X_j(\delta)$, in period $j$ ($j = 0, 1, ..., n$) resulting from a particular decision vector $\delta$. This permits complete generality in specifying the distribution of cash flow as a function of $\delta$. However, the real crux of the problem is to analyze $X_j(\delta)$, to study the interrelationships between the proposed investments, and to thereby develop a model which describes the resulting distribution of $X_j(\delta)$, and therefore of $P(\delta)$, as a function of $\delta$. One such model will be developed in this chapter, with two objectives in mind. First, this model may often be appropriate in its own right for describing the interrelationships between investments and thereby providing a basis for the selection of $\delta$. Second, the development of the model should also serve an illustrative purpose by giving some insight into the nature of alternative formulations that may sometimes be more appropriate.

It will be useful to identify and consider separately the influence of external determinants of cash flow. Examples of such external factors that may influence the amount of cash flow are the general state of the economy, the amount of competition from other firms, price levels for raw materials, new regulations or restrictions imposed by the government, etc. Let $e$ be

---

[1] KENNETH BOULDING (1956).

the number of external determinants of cash flow that are identified. Suppose that there exists an appropriate quantitative measure of each determinant over a time period. For example, Gross National Product could be the measure of the general state of the economy. Let the random variable $V_{jl}$ be the value of the measure (exogenous variable) for the *l*th determinant in time period *j*. Therefore, there exists a function $f_j$, $(j = 1, 2, ..., n)$, such that

$$X_j(\boldsymbol{\delta}) = f_j(V_{j1}, ..., V_{je}, W_j, \boldsymbol{\delta}),$$

where the random variable $W_j$ is a measure of the unidentified sources of variation in cash flow.

**Assumption 1:** The effect of the exogenous variables on cash flow is additive, so that $f_j$ is of the form,

$$f_j(V_{j1}, ..., V_{je}, W_j, \boldsymbol{\delta}) = \sum_{l=1}^{e} g_{jl}(V_{jl}, \boldsymbol{\delta}) + g_j(W_j, \boldsymbol{\delta}), \quad \text{for } j = 1, 2, ..., n.$$

It is possible to trade off the location parameters between the $g_{jl}$ and $g_j$ functions in any arbitrary manner, so it will be assumed without loss of generality that

$$g_{jl}(v_{jl}^*, \boldsymbol{\delta}) = 0 \quad \text{for} \quad j = 1, ..., n; \ l = 1, ..., e; \ \boldsymbol{\delta} \in S,$$

where $v_{jl}^*$ is defined as the smallest median[1] of $V_{jl}$.

In preparation for stating the additional assumptions, define $\boldsymbol{\delta}^{(k)} = (\delta_{1k}, \delta_{2k}, ..., \delta_{mk})$ for $k = 1, ..., m$, where

$$\delta_{jk} = \begin{cases} 0, & \text{if } j \neq k \\ 1, & \text{if } j = k. \end{cases}$$

---

[1] More precisely, $v_{jl}^* = \inf\{v : \text{Prob}\{V_{jl} \geq v\} \geq \frac{1}{2} \leq \text{Prob}\{V_{jl} \leq v\}\}$, Since it is known (see LOÉVE 1960, p. 244) that any random variable either has a unique median or has medians over a closed interval, $v_{jl}^*$ must be a median. The choice of the smallest median was made in order to define a unique value which is also a possible value of $V_{jl}$, so that $g_{jl}$ is defined there. Furthermore, median is an intuitively meaningful concept and is therefore convenient for implementation of the model. Otherwise, the choice was arbitrary and many other methods of assigning location parameters could have been used with a comparable degree of justification.

Define $\sigma_{jkl}^2 = \text{Var}\{g_{jl}(V_{jl}, \delta^{(k)})\}$, so that $\sigma_{jkl}^2$ would be the variance of the change in cash flow in time period $j$ due to the $l$th exogenous variable if investment $k$ were the only one approved.

**Assumption 2:** Let $F_{jkl}(z)$ denote the cumulative distribution function of $g_{jl}(V_{jl}, \delta^{(k)})$ for all $j$, $k$, $l$ $(j = 1, ..., n; k = 1, ..., m; l = 1, ..., e)$. Then for each $j = 1, ..., n$ and $l = 1, ..., e$,

$$F_{j1l}(\sigma_{j1l}z) = F_{j2l}(\sigma_{j2l}z) = ... = F_{jml}(\sigma_{jml}z) \text{ for all } z.$$

In other words, there exists a function $h_{jl}$ $(j = 1, ..., n; l = 1, ..., e)$, such that

$$g_{jl}(V_{jl}, \delta^{(k)}) = \sigma_{jkl}h_{jl}(V_{jl}) \quad \text{for} \quad k = 1, 2, ..., m.$$

Define $Z_{jl} = h_{jl}(V_{jl})$.

**Assumption 3:** $g_{jl}(V_{jl}, \delta) = \sum_{k=1}^{m} \delta_k g_{jl}(V_{jl}, \delta^{(k)})$,

$$\text{for } j = 1, ..., n; l = 1, ..., e.$$

Therefore, Assumptions 2 and 3 imply that

$$g_{jl}(V_{jl}, \delta) = \sum_{k=1}^{m} \delta_k \sigma_{jkl} Z_{jl}, \quad \text{for} \quad j = 1, ..., n; l = 1, ..., e.$$

The cash flow from an investment commonly emanates from a number of distinct sources. For example, an investment may affect sales income, labor costs, maintenance costs, cost of raw materials, etc. It would facilitate determining the pattern of variation of cash flows if these distinct sources were treated separately.

More formally, suppose that $m_k$ mutually exclusive and exhaustive sources of cash flow emanating from the $k$th investment are identified. Let the random variable $Y_{jkl}$ $(j = 1, ..., n; k = 1, ..., m; l = 1, ..., m_k)$ be the cash flow in period $j$ from the $l$th source for the $k$th investment, given $\delta = \delta^{(k)}$ and $V_{jt} = v_{jt}^*$ for $t = 1, 2, ..., e$. Thus, $Y_{jkl}$ is the cash flow from a particular source if only the $k$th investment is made and all the exogenous variables are "neutral" in the sense that they take on their median values.

Since

$$g_j(W_j, \delta) = f(v_{j1}^*, ..., v_{je}^*, W_j, \delta),$$

$g_j(W_j, \delta)$ is the cash flow in period $j$ resulting from the decision $\delta$ when all the exogenous variables are neutral. Therefore,

$$g_j(W_j, \delta^{(k)}) = \sum_{l=1}^{m_k} Y_{jkl}$$

by definition.

The remaining question concerns the nature of the competitive or complementary effect when investments are made in combination with each other.

**Assumption 4:** The competitive or complementary effect of joint investments on total net cash flow is deterministic and additive. In other words, there exists a function $h_j(\delta)$ such that

$$g_j(W_j, \delta) = \sum_{k=1}^{m} \sum_{l=1}^{m_k} \delta_k Y_{jkl} + h_j(\delta), \quad \text{for} \quad j = 1, ..., n; \ \delta \in S.$$

To summarize, Assumptions 1, 2, 3, and 4 yield

$$X_j(\delta) = \sum_{k=1}^{m} \sum_{l=1}^{m_k} \delta_k Y_{jkl} + h_j(\delta) + \sum_{l=1}^{e} \sum_{k=1}^{m} \delta_k \sigma_{jkl} Z_{jl}, \quad \text{for} \quad j = 1, ..., n.$$

This decomposition of $X_j(\delta)$ was designed to reduce it into its simplest elements. Each of the terms should be amenable to a relatively simple intuitive interpretation. Sections 4.1 and 6.1 discuss the use of this model to determine $E\{P(\delta)\}$ and $\text{Var}\{P(\delta)\}$. The Appendix discusses procedures for estimating the input parameters.

Since $X_0(\delta)$ is immediate cash flow, presumably the immediate negative cash outlay for the investments, it would usually be known with certainty (and this is assumed henceforth). Therefore, it would seldom be fruitful to decompose $X_0(\delta)$, and it will not be done here. A method for doing so, when it is desired, is suggested by the preceding work, although a much less refined decomposition should suffice.

# CHAPTER 4

# PROBABILITY DISTRIBUTION OF PRESENT VALUE

## 4.1. Non-parametric analysis

Before investigating the functional form of the probability distribution of $P(\delta)$ (which will be done in Section 4.2), it would be well to determine what conclusions can be drawn, if any, without any knowledge of the distribution other than $E\{P(\delta)\}$ and $\mathrm{Var}\{P(\delta)\}$.

If the analyst understands the meaning and significance of expected values and standard deviations, knowledge of $E\{P(\delta)\}$ and $\mathrm{Var}\{P(\delta)\}$ for various $\delta$ provides a fairly substantial basis for a subjective comparison of these $\delta$ vectors. Several types of calculations could be made to aid in this comparison. One such type would concern upper bounds on the amount of risk involved. The well-known Tchebycheff inequality yields

$$\mathrm{Prob}\{|P(\delta) - E\{P(\delta)\}| \geqslant k\sqrt{\mathrm{Var}\{P(\delta)\}}\} \leqslant k^{-2}$$

for all $k$ regardless of the distribution of $P(\delta)$. Thus, for example, the probability is no more than 0.25, 0.04, and 0.01, respectively, that $P(\delta)$ will be less than $E\{P(\delta)\} - 2\sqrt{\mathrm{Var}\{P(\delta)\}}$, $E\{P(\delta)\} - 5\sqrt{\mathrm{Var}\{P(\delta)\}}$, and $E\{P(\delta)\} - 10\sqrt{\mathrm{Var}\{P(\delta)\}}$, respectively. However, the Tchebycheff inequality usually is very conservative. Thus, if the distribution of $P(\delta)$ actually is normal, the probability is only 0.0014 that $P(\delta)$ will be less than $E\{P(\delta)\} - 3\sqrt{\mathrm{Var}\{P(\delta)\}}$. For most distributions, it is "very unlikely" that a given observation will lie below the mean minus three standard deviations. Therefore, the risk associated with $\delta$ may be partially described by using the Tchebycheff inequality, but these results should be tempered by comparison with calculations for the normal distribution where $E\{P(\delta)\} - 3\sqrt{\text{Var}\{P(\delta)\}}$ may be considered as almost a lower bound on $P(\delta)$. An evaluation of both the risk and expected present value associated with various $\delta$ vectors should enable the analyst to make a reasonable selection of $\delta$.

If the model of cash flows given in Chapter 3 were being used, and if the necessary input information were available, the mean and variance of $P(\delta)$ would be obtained as follows.

$$E\{P(\delta)\} = X_0 + \sum_{j=1}^{n} \frac{E\{X_j(\delta)\}}{\prod_{k=1}^{j}(1+i_k(\delta))},$$

where

$$E\{(X_j(\delta)\} = \sum_{k=1}^{m}\sum_{l=1}^{m_k} \delta_k E(Y_{jkl}) + h_j(\delta) + \sum_{l=1}^{e}\sum_{k=1}^{m} \delta_k \sigma_{jkl} E(Z_{jl}),$$

$$\text{for } j = 1, ..., n.$$

To find $\text{Var}\{P(\delta)\}$, begin by constructing the covariance matrix for $Y_{jkl}$ and $Z_{jl}$ $(j=1, ..., n; k=1, ..., m; l=1, ... m_k)$. Multiply both the row and column corresponding to $Y_{jkl}$ by $\left[\delta_k \Big/ \prod_{t=1}^{j}(1+i_t(\delta))\right]$ for $j = 1, ..., n;$ $k = 1, ..., m;$ $l = 1, ..., m_k$. Multiply both the row and column corresponding to $Z_{jl}$ by $\left[\sum_{k=1}^{m} \delta_k \sigma_{jkl} \Big/ \prod_{k=1}^{j}(1+i_k(\delta))\right]$ for $j = 1, ..., n; l = 1, ..., e$. $\text{Var}\{P(\delta)\}$ is just the sum of the elements of this modified covariance matrix. If the $i_k(\delta)$ are constants independent of $\delta$, it is expeditious to combine all of the coefficients of each $\delta_k$ (as demonstrated in Section 6.1) before calculating $E\{P(\delta)\}$ and $\text{Var}\{P(\delta)\}$ for a series of values of $\delta$.

## 4.2. The central limit problem

The non-parametric analysis discussed in the last section is not very precise. It requires much subjective evaluation and is unable to explicitly use the information contained in the utility function of total present value. Therefore, it would be extremely helpful to obtain the actual probability distribution of $P(\delta)$, since this would enable one, in principle, to find $E\{U(P(\delta))\}$ and to thereby find the $\delta$ which maximizes expected utility. It would be especially welcome if this distribution were to happen to be normal, since this would allow using all of the results of Chapter 2. This section will be devoted to discussing the conditions under which $P(\delta)$ is normal or approximately normal.

One immediate conclusion is that $P(\delta)$ is normal whenever the joint distribution of $X_1(\delta)$, $X_2(\delta)$, ..., $X_n(\delta)$ is multivariate normal. This follows from the well-known fact (e.g., see ANDERSON 1958, pp. 19–27) that the distribution of any linear combination of random variables is normal if their joint distribution is multivariate normal. This fact would also imply that, if the model of cash flows from Chapter 3 were being used, $P(\delta)$ would be normal whenever the joint distribution of $Y_{jkl}$ $(j=1, ..., n; k=1, ..., m; l=1, ..., m_k)$ and $Z_{jl}$ $(j=1, ..., n; l=1, ..., e)$ is multivariate normal.

The more challenging and interesting question concerns the case where $X_j(\delta)$ is non-normal. $P(\delta)$ is the sum of a number of random variables, $\left[ X_j(\delta) \Big/ \prod_{k=1}^{j} (1+i_k(\delta)) \right]$ for $j = 0, 1, ..., n$, where each of these random variables may itself be the sum of random variables such as $Y_{jkl}$ and $Z_{jl}$ of Chapter 3. It is known that, under certain conditions, the distribution of the sum of random variables is asymptotically normal, so that the distribution of the sum of a large finite number of these random variables should be approximately normal. Therefore, $P(\delta)$ should be approximately normal if these conditions hold for the random variables whose sum is $P(\delta)$. A discussion of these conditions follows.

The "Central Limit Problem" (the name given to the problem of determining the above conditions) is one of the most important problems of probability theory, and many sets of sufficient conditions for the Central Limit Theorem to hold have been and are being developed. The reader is referred to any book on advanced probability theory, e.g., LOÉVE (1960), for a partial resume. The best-known version of the Central Limit Theorem states that, if $W_1, W_2, ...$ are independent, identically distributed (non-degenerate) random variables (with finite mean and variance), then (after suitable normalization) their sum is asymptotically normal. However, the random variables in the present problem are neither independent nor identically distributed in general. Fortunately, much weaker conditions have been discovered. For the case of independent random variables with finite means and variances, the following complete solution of the Central Limit Problem has been obtained. A sequence $\{W_k\}$ obeys the Central Limit Theorem if and only if, for every $\varepsilon > 0$, the truncated random variables $T_k$ defined by

$$T_k = W_k \quad \text{if} \quad |W_k| \leqslant \varepsilon s_n$$
$$T_k = 0 \quad \text{if} \quad |W_k| > \varepsilon s_n \,,$$

$(k = 1, 2, \ldots, n)$ satisfy the condition,

$$\lim_{n \to \infty} \frac{\operatorname{Var}(T_1 + \ldots + T_n)}{s_n^2} = 1 \quad \text{and} \quad \lim_{n \to \infty} s_n = \infty \,,[1]$$

where $s_n^2$ denotes $\operatorname{Var}(W_1 + \ldots + W_n)$. One important implication of this result is that every uniformly bounded non-degenerate sequence of mutually independent random variables obeys the Central Limit Theorem. Uniform boundedness would seem to be a weak condition for the investment problem under consideration. Surprisingly, the non-degeneracy condition may be more restrictive. For example, suppose that $\operatorname{Var}\{X_j(\delta)\} = \sigma^2$ and $\dfrac{1}{1 + i_j(\delta)} = \alpha$ for all $j$. Then $P(\delta) = \sum\limits_{j=0}^{n} \alpha^j X_j(\delta)$, but $\lim\limits_{n \to \infty} \operatorname{Var}\left\{\sum\limits_{j=0}^{n} \alpha^j X_j(\delta)\right\} = \dfrac{\sigma^2}{1 - \alpha^2} < \infty$ so $\lim\limits_{n \to \infty} \left\{\sum\limits_{j=0}^{n} \alpha^j X_j(\delta)\right\}$ is not normal if $X_j(\delta)$ is not normal. On the other hand, it may be possible to circumvent this discounting problem by decomposing $X_j(\delta)$ such as in Chapter 3 and applying the Central Limit Theorem to the random variables whose sum is $X_j(\delta)$. Finally, it should be noted that the independence assumption is very restrictive.

A number of Central Limit Theorems for dependent random variables have been developed. Unfortunately, the dependent case is very much more

---

[1] The fact that this condition is necessary and sufficient was proved by Feller and Lindeberg, respectively. See FELLER (1957) for a discussion and references.

difficult than the independent case, so that it will not be possible to state a single result which completely solves this problem. However, several relevant results can be stated.

In general terms, rigorous theorems are available which allow "some" dependence if the random variables are identically distributed; certain patterns of non-identical distributions are also allowed for more restricted patterns of dependence.

DOOB (1953) discusses a Central Limit Theorem for stationary Markov processes which would be relevant for this problem when $\left\{ \dfrac{X_j(\delta)}{\prod\limits_{k=1}^{j}(1+i_k(\delta))} \right\}$

is a stationary sequence of Markov-dependent random variables. This theorem is quite involved, so only the special case relevant for this problem will be stated. Let $W_1$, $W_2$, ... be a sequence of Markov-dependent random variables. Assume that they are identically distributed with mean $\mu$ and variance $\sigma^2$. Assume additionally that the conditional distribution of $W_{j+1}$, given $W_j$, is the same for $j = 1, 2, \ldots$, that the density function for the conditional distribution is strictly positive wherever the density function for the unconditional distribution is strictly positive, and that there exists an $\varepsilon > 0$ such that the mass in the conditional distribution is less than $(1 - \varepsilon)$ wherever the mass in the unconditional distribution is less than $\varepsilon$. Under these conditions, the general statement of the theorem implies that the distribution of $\sum\limits_{j=1}^{N} \dfrac{W_j - \mu}{\sqrt{N}}$ converges to a normal distribution with mean zero and variance $\sigma^2$.

The primary shortcoming in the above result is the requirement that the random variables be identically distributed. Under independence, it was possible to greatly relax this requirement and to assume only, in effect, that no individual random variables had such large variances relative to the others that their distributions dominated the distribution of the sum. However, adding the complication of dependence has meant that it has heretofore been possible only to prove much more modest results of this type. One of these results is the following.

Let $W_1$, $W_2$, ... be a sequence of random variables. Assume that this sequence is $q$-dependent, i.e., $(W_1, \ldots, W_r)$ is always independent of $(W_s, W_{s+1}, \ldots)$ if $s - r > q$. Define

$$A_j = 2 \sum_{k=0}^{q-1} \text{Cov}\{W_{j+k}, W_{j+q}\} + \text{Var}\{W_{j+q}\} \ .$$

Assume $E\{W_j\} = 0$ and $E\{|W_j|^3\} \leqslant T^3 < \infty$ for $j = 1, 2, \dots$. Assume that the limit

$$\lim_{p \to \infty} \frac{1}{p} \sum_{k=1}^{p} A_{j+k} = A$$

exists uniformly for all $j$. Then the Hoeffding and Robbins Theorem (HOEFFDING and ROBBINS 1948; FRASER 1957) states that $\sum_{j=1}^{N} W_j$ is asymptotically normal with mean 0 and variance NA. Hoeffding and Robbins have also proven a direct multivariate extension of this univariate theorem.

It appears quite possible that the Hoeffding and Robbins Theorem will occasionally be applicable to the investment problem under consideration. The condition that $E\{|W_j|^3\} \leqslant T^3 < \infty$ for $j = 1, 2, \dots$ would be fulfilled if the random variables involved are uniformly bounded. The $E\{W_j\} = 0$ condition is not essential since location parameters would not be relevant to the question of the normality of $P(\delta)$. The requirement that the specified limit should exist implies a certain degree of uniformity and consistency in the pattern of variances and covariances in the sequence. The remaining requirement of $q$-dependence does not seem overly severe.

Other Central Limit results for the case of dependent random variables have also been obtained. See LOÉVE (1960, p. 377) for example. However, a complete solution to the Central Limit Problem for this case is not yet available.

The above results indicate the conditions under which $P(\delta)$ would be "approximately" normal. It is now time to face the question of the goodness of the approximation. The problem is that, even when the Central Limit Theorem applies, there is no guarantee that the rate of convergence to normality is sufficiently rapid that the distribution of the finite sum yielding $P(\delta)$ will yet be reasonably close to normal. For the case of completely independent random variables, it is known that a small number of them will suffice to yield a reasonable approximation of normality. The field of statistical quality control has traditionally relied on 4 or 5 for setting control limits on Shewhart $\bar{X}$ control charts (e.g., see GRANT 1952). Not as much is known about the case of dependent random variables, although it seems evident that a larger number usually would be required. The magnitude of the required number would depend upon the degree and type of dependence. An additional factor is the distribution of the individual random variables. If their distributions somewhat resemble the normal distribution, one would have greater confidence that their sum would be approximately normal.

To summarize, $P(\delta)$ has a normal distribution whenever the joint distribution of $X_1(\delta)$, $X_2(\delta)$, ..., $X_n(\delta)$ is multivariate normal. Otherwise, the distribution of $P(\delta)$ will still be approximately normal if certain conditions described above are satisfied.

## 4.3. Non-utilitarian analysis

Before proceeding to Chapter 5 and the derivation of $E\{U(P(\delta))\}$, it should be noted that knowledge of the probability distribution of $P(\delta)$ for all $\delta \in S$ provides a substantial basis for a subjective selection of $\delta$. An earlier paper by this writer (HILLIER 1963) focused on how this might be done, thereby eliminating the necessity of constructing an utility function. It was pointed out that, from a practical point of view, the management of a firm often would have neither the time nor the inclination to participate in the task of constructing their utility function. On the other hand, knowledge of the distribution of $P(\delta)$ enables management to quickly apply the procedure of evaluating expected utility in an intuitive and implicit sense.

# CHAPTER 5

# EXPECTED UTILITY

## 5.1. An approximate solution under normality

When $U(p)$ is a continuous function, it may be approximated as closely as desired by a continuous piece-wise quadratic function. (In practice, this latter function probably would be constructed by approximating the marginal utility function $U'(p)$ by a piece-wise linear function.) Therefore, in order to derive a value which is arbitrarily close to $E\{U(P(\delta))\}$, it will be sufficient to find the expected value of a continuous piece-wise quadratic function. Thus, let the number $M$, the monotonic increasing sequence of numbers $\{-\infty, p_1, p_2, ..., p_{M-1}, +\infty)$, and the three unrestricted sequences of numbers, $\{a_1, a_2, ..., a_M\}, \{b_1, b_2, ..., b_M\}$, and $\{c_1, c_2, ..., c_M\}$, be such that

$$U(p) = \tfrac{1}{2} a_j p^2 + b_j p + c_j + g(p), \quad \text{if} \quad p_{j-1} \leqslant p \leqslant p_j,$$

for $j = 1, 2, ..., M$ ($p_0 \equiv -\infty, p_M \equiv +\infty$), where $g(p)$ is some function bounded in absolute value by a specified positive constant $\varepsilon$. (To correspond to the convention adopted in Section 1.4, it is further specified that $b_j = 1$, $c_j = 0$ if $p_{j-1} \leqslant 0 \leqslant p_j$.)

The following derivation will indicate how to find the expected utility, $E\{U(P(\delta))\}$, if $P(\delta)$ has a normal distribution. Thus, when $P(\delta)$ is approximately normal according to the analysis of Section 4.2, this procedure should provide a reasonable approximation of $E\{U(P(\delta))\}$.

Assume $P(\delta)$ has a normal distribution. To expedite the following work, $E\{P(\delta)\}$ and $\text{Var}\{P(\delta)\}$ will be denoted by $\mu$ and $\sigma^2$, respectively.

Then,

$$f(p) = \frac{1}{\sqrt{2\pi}\,\sigma}\, e^{-\frac{p-\mu}{2\sigma^2}}$$

is the probability density function of $P(\delta)$. Therefore,

$$E\{U(P(\delta))\} = \int_{-\infty}^{\infty} U(p)f(p)\,dp$$

$$= \sum_{j=1}^{M} \int_{p_{j-1}}^{p_j} [\tfrac{1}{2}a_j p^2 + b_j p + c_j + g(p)]f(p)\,dp$$

$$= \sum_{j=1}^{M} \left[ \tfrac{1}{2}a_j \int_{p_{j-1}}^{p_j} p^2 f(p)\,dp + b_j \int_{p_{j-1}}^{p_j} pf(p)\,dp \right.$$

$$\left. + c_j \int_{p_{j-1}}^{p_j} f(p)\,dp \right] + \beta,$$

where $|\beta| \leqslant \varepsilon$.

The last integral can be readily evaluated by the use of a cumulative normal probability table. The problem is therefore reduced to finding $\int_{p_{j-1}}^{p_j} p^2 f(p)\,dp$ and $\int_{p_{j-1}}^{p_j} pf(p)\,dp$. The following equivalent problem will

be solved. Assume that $W_j$ is distributed according to a truncated normal distribution. More precisely, assume that the probability density function of $W_j$ is

$$g(w) = \begin{cases} \dfrac{1}{\text{Prob}\{p_{j-1} \leqslant P(\delta) \leqslant p_j\}} f(p), & \text{if } p_{j-1} \leqslant p \leqslant p_j \\ 0 & , \text{otherwise.} \end{cases}$$

The problem is to find $E(W_j)$ and $E(W_j^2)$. This is equivalent to the original problem since

$$\int_{p_{j-1}}^{p_j} pf(p)\,dp = \text{Prob}\{p_{j-1} \leqslant P(\delta) \leqslant p_j\}\, E(W_j)$$

and

$$\int_{p_{j-1}}^{p_j} p^2 f(p)\,dp = \text{Prob}\{p_{j-1} \leqslant P(\delta) \leqslant p_j\}\, E(W_j^2).$$

The usual symbols, $\varphi(\cdot)$ and $\Phi(\cdot)$, will be used to denote the probability density function and the cumulative distribution function, respectively, for a normal distribution with mean zero and variance one. The moment-generating function of $W_j$, $E(e^{tW_j})$, will be denoted as $m_{W_j}(t)$. The well-known property (e.g., see MOOD 1950, p. 102) of moment-generating functions is that

$$E(W_j) = m'_{W_j}(0)$$

and

$$E(W_j^2) = m''_{W_j}(0).$$

To begin, $m_{W_j}(t)$ must be found as follows.

$$m_{W_j}(t) = E(e^{tW_j}) = e^{t\mu} E(e^{t(W_j-\mu)})$$

$$= e^{t\mu} \int_{p_{j-1}}^{p_j} \frac{1}{\text{Prob}\{p_{j-1} \leqslant P(\delta) \leqslant p_j\}} \frac{1}{\sqrt{2\pi}\sigma} e^{t(w-\mu)} e^{-\frac{(w-\mu)^2}{2\sigma^2}} dw$$

$$= e^{t\mu + \frac{\sigma^2 t^2}{2}} \frac{1}{\text{Prob}\{p_{j-1} \leqslant P(\delta) \leqslant p_j\}} \frac{1}{\sqrt{2\pi}\sigma} \int_{p_{j-1}}^{p_j} e^{-\frac{(w-\mu-\sigma^2 t)^2}{2\sigma^2}} dw$$

$$= \frac{e^{t\mu + \frac{\sigma^2 t^2}{2}}}{\text{Prob}\{p_{j-1} \leqslant P(\delta) \leqslant p_j\}} \left[\Phi\left(\frac{p_j - \mu}{\sigma} - \sigma t\right) - \Phi\left(\frac{p_{j-1} - \mu}{\sigma} - \sigma t\right)\right].$$

Therefore,

$$\text{Prob}\{p_{j-1} \leqslant P(\delta) \leqslant p_j\} m'_{W_j}(t) =$$

$$= e^{t\mu + \frac{\sigma^2 t^2}{2}} \left[-\sigma\varphi\left(\frac{p_j - \mu}{\sigma} - \sigma t\right) + \sigma\varphi\left(\frac{p_{j-1} - \mu}{\sigma} - \sigma t\right)\right]$$

$$+ (\mu + \sigma^2 t) e^{t\mu + \frac{\sigma^2 t^2}{2}} \left[\Phi\left(\frac{p_j - \mu}{\sigma} - \sigma t\right) - \Phi\left(\frac{p_{j-1} - \mu}{\sigma} - \sigma t\right)\right],$$

so that

$$\int_{p_{j-1}}^{p_j} pf(p)\,dp = \text{Prob}\{p_{j-1} \leqslant P(\delta) \leqslant p_j\}\, m'_{W_j}(0)$$

$$= \left[-\sigma\varphi\left(\frac{p_j-\mu}{\sigma}\right) + \sigma\varphi\left(\frac{p_{j-1}-\mu}{\sigma}\right)\right] + \mu\left[\Phi\left(\frac{p_j-\mu}{\sigma}\right) - \Phi\left(\frac{p_{j-1}-\mu}{\sigma}\right)\right].$$

Furthermore,

$$\text{Prob}\{p_{j-1} \leqslant P(\delta) \leqslant p_j\}\, m''_{W_j}(t)$$

$$= e^{t\mu + \frac{\sigma^2 t^2}{2}}\left[\sigma^2\varphi'\left(\frac{p_j-\mu}{\sigma} - \sigma t\right) - \sigma^2\varphi'\left(\frac{p_{j-1}-\mu}{\sigma} - \sigma t\right)\right]$$

$$+ (\mu+\sigma^2 t)e^{t\mu + \frac{\sigma^2 t^2}{2}}\left[-\sigma\varphi\left(\frac{p_j-\mu}{\sigma} - \sigma t\right) + \sigma\varphi\left(\frac{p_{j-1}-\mu}{\sigma} - \sigma t\right)\right]$$

$$+ (\mu+\sigma^2 t)e^{t\mu + \frac{\sigma^2 t^2}{2}}\left[-\sigma\varphi\left(\frac{p_j-\mu}{\sigma} - \sigma t\right) + \sigma\varphi\left(\frac{p_{j-1}-\mu}{\sigma} - \sigma t\right)\right]$$

$$+ [(\mu+\sigma^2 t)^2 + \sigma^2]e^{t\mu + \frac{\sigma^2 t^2}{2}}\left[\Phi\left(\frac{p_j-\mu}{\sigma} - \sigma t\right) - \Phi\left(\frac{p_{j-1}-\mu}{\sigma} - \sigma t\right)\right],$$

so that

$$\int_{p_{j-1}}^{p} p^2 f(p)\,dp = \text{Prob}\{p_{j-1} \leqslant P(\delta) \leqslant p_j\}\, m''_{W_j}(0)$$

$$= \sigma^2\left[\varphi'\left(\frac{p_j-\mu}{\sigma}\right) - \varphi'\left(\frac{p_{j-1}-\mu}{\sigma}\right)\right] - 2\mu\sigma\left[\varphi\left(\frac{p_j-\mu}{\sigma}\right)\right.$$

$$\left. - \varphi\left(\frac{p_{j-1}-\mu}{\sigma}\right)\right] + (\mu^2+\sigma^2)\left[\Phi\left(\frac{p_j-\mu}{\sigma}\right) - \Phi\left(\frac{p_{j-1}-\mu}{\sigma}\right)\right],$$

where

$$\varphi'\left(\frac{p_j-\mu}{\sigma}\right) = -\left(\frac{p_j-\mu}{\sigma}\right)\frac{1}{\sqrt{2\pi}\,\sigma}\,e^{-\frac{(p_j-\mu)^2}{2\sigma^2}}$$

## 5.2. A general solution for a certain class of utility functions

This section will derive $E\{U(P(\delta))\}$ by using a Taylor series expansion of $U(p)$ about $E\{P(\delta)\}$.

Assume that $U(p)$ has a finite $N$th derivative $U^{(N)}(p)$ for all $p$ and that $U^{(N-1)}(p)$ is continuous everywhere. Then Taylor's Theorem (APOSTOL 1957, p. 96) states that, for any $p^*$ and every $p \neq p^*$, there exists a point $\xi$ interior to the interval joining $p$ and $p^*$ such that

$$U(p) = U(p^*) + \sum_{k=1}^{N-1}\frac{U^{(k)}(p^*)}{k!}(p-p^*)^k + \frac{U^{(N)}(\xi)}{N!}(p-p^*)^N .$$

Denote $\mu = E\{P(\delta)\}$ and let $p^* = \mu$. Then if the hypothesis holds for all $N$,

$$E\{U(P(\delta))\} = U(\mu) + \sum_{k=1}^{\infty}\frac{U^{(k)}(\mu)}{k!}E\{(P(\delta)-\mu)^k\} .$$

Since

$$E\{P(\delta) - \mu\} = 0$$

and

$$E\{(P(\delta)-\mu)^2\} = \mathrm{Var}\{P(\delta)\} ,$$

(which is hereafter denoted by $\sigma^2$), this expression reduces to

$$E\{U(P(\delta))\} = U(\mu) + \frac{U^{(2)}(\mu)}{2}\sigma^2 + \sum_{k=3}^{\infty}\frac{U^{(k)}(\mu)}{k!}E\{(P(\delta)-\mu)^k\} .$$

Therefore, if the summation term is small, a very useful approximation of $E\{U(P(\delta))\}$ is

$$E\{U(P(\delta))\} \doteq U(\mu) + \frac{U^{(2)}(\mu)}{2}\sigma^2 .$$

Similarly, if the hypothesis holds at least for $N = 3$, it is likewise true that

$$E\{U(P(\delta))\} = U(\mu) + \frac{U^{(2)}(\mu)}{2}\sigma^2 + R \ ,$$

where the remainder term $R$ is

$$R = \int_{-\infty}^{\infty} \frac{U^{(3)}(\xi(p))}{6}(p-\mu)^3 f(p)dp \ ,$$

where $f(p)$ is the probability density function of $P(\delta)$ and $\xi(p)$ is the value between $p$ and $\mu$ defined by Taylor's Theorem for $N=3$. Thus,

$$|R| \leqslant \frac{E\{|(P(\delta)-\mu)^3|\}}{6}\left[\sup_{-\infty < \xi < \infty}\{|U^{(3)}(\xi)|\}\right],$$

which establishes an upper bound on the error if the remainder term $R$ is ignored.

If one is willing to use the approximation developed above, the problem reduces to maximizing $f(\mu, \sigma^2) = U(\mu) + \dfrac{U^{(2)}(\mu)}{2}\sigma^2$ over $(\mu, \sigma^2)$ corresponding to $\delta \in S$. It may be more suggestive to rewrite $f(\mu, \sigma^2)$ as

$$f(\mu, \sigma^2) = f_1(\mu)\mu - f_2(\mu)\sigma^2 \ , \quad [1]$$

where

$$f_1(\mu) = \frac{U(\mu)}{\mu} \ , \quad f_2(\mu) = \frac{-U^{(2)}(\mu)}{2} \ .$$

Thus, if one were to plot a family of curves of the form, $f(\mu, \sigma^2) = c$, on a graph with $\mu$ and $\sigma^2$ as the axes, these would constitute a family of indifference curves. The objective would be to find the feasible point whose indifference curve is furthest away from the origin (in the positive quadrant). Thus, one is willing to increase $\sigma^2$ while simultaneously

---

[1] FARRAR (1962) also exhibits this approximation. However, he then proceeds to translate the utility function origin in order to write it as $\mu + \dfrac{U^{(2)}(\mu)}{2}\sigma^2$. While this may be done with each $\delta$ individually, the required translation is different for different $\delta$, so $\mu + \dfrac{U^{(2)}(\mu)}{2}\sigma^2$ is not a valid objective function, given the preceding formulation.

increasing $\mu$ as long as the total differential of $f(\mu, \sigma^2)$ is positive. Letting $z = f(\mu, \sigma^2)$, the total differential is

$$dz = \frac{\partial z}{\partial \mu} d\mu + \frac{\partial z}{\partial \sigma^2} d\sigma^2$$

$$= \left[ U^{(1)}(\mu) + \frac{U^{(3)}(\mu)}{2} \sigma^2 \right] d\mu + \frac{U^{(2)}(\mu)}{2} d\sigma^2 .$$

Therefore,

$$dz > 0 \quad \text{if} \quad \frac{d\mu}{d\sigma^2} > \frac{-U^{(2)}(\mu)/2}{U^{(1)}(\mu) + \dfrac{U^{(3)}(\mu)}{2} \sigma^2} .$$

Thus, if $\Delta\mu$ and $\Delta\sigma^2$ are positive quantities, $(\mu+\Delta\mu, \sigma^2+\Delta\sigma^2)$ is preferred to $(\mu, \sigma^2)$ if and only if the line integral,

$$\int_{(\mu,\sigma^2)}^{(\mu+\Delta\mu,\sigma^2+\Delta\sigma^2)} dz > 0 ,$$

i.e., if and only if one climbs to a higher indifference curve by increasing $\mu$ and $\sigma^2$ by $\Delta\mu$ and $\Delta\sigma^2$, respectively. It is evident that a sufficient condition for this to hold is that

$$\frac{\Delta\mu}{\Delta\sigma^2} > \frac{-U^{(2)}(\mu+k\Delta\mu)/2}{U^{(1)}(\mu+k\Delta\mu) + \dfrac{U^{(3)}(\mu+k\Delta\mu)}{2} (\sigma^2+k\Delta\sigma^2)} \quad \text{if} \quad 0 \leqslant k \leqslant 1 .$$

Each of the next two sections will formulate and investigate a special case of the class of utility functions assumed in this section.

## 5.3. A hyperbola model

In order to use all of the results of Chapter 2 and Section 5.2, it is necessary to have a monotonic increasing concave utility function which possesses a finite third derivative everywhere. While this requirement corresponds to one's intuitive notion of how most utility functions should behave, it may not be trivial to construct such a non-linear function algebraically.

For example, a concave quadratic function necessarily bends down if the argument is sufficiently large and so is not monotonic increasing. The piece-wise quadratic function assumed in Section 5.1 may fail since it need not possess derivatives at the break points. Thus, the problem is a purely technical one of constructing a function algebraically which behaves in the desired way. One class of functions of this type will be developed in this section.

A crucial question is what happens to $U(p)$ when $p$ becomes very large positively or negatively. One alternative answer which seems plausible is that $U(p)$ converges to linear asymptotes. (In other words, the marginal utility function $U'(p)$ converges to a constant as $p$ increases in either the positive or the negative direction.) This would indicate that $U(p)$ is a hyperbola, so that $U(p)$ satisfies an equation of the form,

$$Ap^2 + BpU(p) + CU^2(p) + Dp + EU(p) + F = 0 .$$

Following is a derivation of the values of these parameters, given the asymptotes.

Let the specified asymptotes be $a_1 + b_1 p$ and $a_2 + b_2 p$, where $a_1 > 0$, $0 \leqslant b_1 < 1$, $a_2 > 0$, and $b_2 > 1$ (one additional restriction will be imposed on $a_1, b_1, a_2, b_2$ subsequently). There exists a family of hyperbolas which possess these asymptotes. However, only one of these hyperbolas also obeys the convention introduced in Section 1.4 that $U(p)$ passes through the origin with slope one. The requirement that $U(0) = 0$ immediately implies that

$$F = 0 .$$

The requirement that $U'(0) = 1$ will be applied after deriving $U'(p)$.

$$2Apdp + BpdU(p) + BU(p)dp + 2CU(p)dU(p) + Ddp + EdU(p) = 0 ,$$

so that

$$(Bp + 2CU(p) + E)dU(p) = -(2Ap + BU(p) + D)dp .$$

Therefore,

$$U'(p) = \frac{-(2Ap + BU(p) + D)}{Bp + 2CU(p) + E} .$$

Hence, $U'(0)=1$ and $U(0)=0$ implies that

$$D = -E.$$

The information about the asymptotes will now be used. Notice that

$$CU^2(p)+(Bp+E)\,U(p)+(Ap^2+Dp)=0.$$

Adopt the convention that $C>0$, which may be done arbitrarily for a homogeneous equation. Therefore,

$$U(p) = \frac{-(Bp+E)-\sqrt{(Bp+E)^2-4C(Ap^2+Dp)}}{2C}.$$

(The square root term is preceded by a $-$ sign rather than $\pm$ because the desired hyperbola has a twin on the other side of the asymptotes which is given by the $+$ sign.) Since

$$\lim_{p\to\infty}\{U(p)-b_1 p\}=a_1,$$

then

$$\lim_{p\to\infty}\left\{\frac{-(Bp+E)-\sqrt{(Bp+E)^2-4C(Ap^2+Dp)}}{2C}-b_1 p\right\}=a_1.$$

$$\sqrt{(Bp+E)^2-4C(Ap^2+Dp)}=\sqrt{(B^2-4CA)p^2+(2BE-4CD)p+E^2}$$

$$=\sqrt{\left[(B^2-4CA)^{\frac12}p+\frac{BE-2CD}{(B^2-4CA)^{\frac12}}\right]^2+E^2-\frac{(BE-2CD)^2}{B^2-4CA}}$$

$$\sim (B^2-4CA)^{\frac12}p+\frac{BE-2CD}{(B^2-4CA)^{\frac12}}.$$

(Here the sign $\sim$ indicates that the ratio of the two sides converges to unity.) Therefore,

$$\frac{-E-\dfrac{BE-2CD}{(B^2-4CA)^{\frac12}}}{2C}+\left[\frac{-B-(B^2-4CA)^{\frac12}}{2C}-b_1\right]\lim_{p\to\infty}p=a_1,$$

which implies that

$$-E - \frac{\dfrac{BE-2CD}{(B^2-4CA)^{\frac{1}{2}}}}{2C} = a_1$$

and

$$\frac{-B-(B^2-4CA)^{\frac{1}{2}}}{2C} - b_1 = 0 \, .$$

To obtain the corresponding equations for the other asymptote, use

$$\lim_{p\to-\infty} \{U(p)-b_2 p\} = a_2 \, .$$

Proceed just as before, except that this time, as $p \to -\infty$,

$$\sqrt{(Bp+E)^2-4C(Ap^2+Dp)} \underset{p\to-\infty}{\sim} -(B^2-4CA)^{\frac{1}{2}}p + \frac{BE-2CD}{-(B^2-4CA)^{\frac{1}{2}}} \, .$$

(The minus branch of $\pm(B^2-4CA)^{\frac{1}{2}}$ is the proper one in this case since it yields the desired hyperbola rather than its twin.) Therefore,

$$\frac{-E + \dfrac{BE-2CD}{(B^2-4CA)^{\frac{1}{2}}}}{2C} + \left[\frac{-B+(B^2-4CA)^{\frac{1}{2}}}{2C} - b_2\right] \lim_{p\to-\infty} p = a_2 \, ,$$

which implies that

$$\frac{-E + \dfrac{BE-2CD}{(B^2-4CA)^{\frac{1}{2}}}}{2C} = a_2$$

and

$$\frac{-B+(B^2-4CA)^{\frac{1}{2}}}{2C} - b_2 = 0 \, .$$

The final equations involving $b_1$ and $b_2$ together imply that

$$-B = (b_1+b_2)C$$

and

$$(B^2-4AC)^{\frac{1}{2}} = (b_2-b_1)C \, .$$

The final equations involving $a_1$ and $a_2$ together imply that

$$-E = (a_1 + a_2)C$$

and

$$\frac{BE - 2CD}{(B^2 - 4CA)^{\frac{1}{2}}} = (a_2 - a_1)C .$$

The first two results together imply that

$$A = \frac{(b_1 + b_2)^2 - (b_2 - b_1)^2}{4} C$$

$$= b_1 b_2 C .$$

The third result, and the result that $D = -E$, yields

$$D = (a_1 + a_2)C .$$

Finally, the fourth result and others imply that

$$C^2(b_1 + b_2)(a_1 + a_2) - 2C^2(a_1 + a_2) = C^2(a_2 - a_1)(b_2 - b_1) ,$$

which reduces to

$$a_1 b_2 + a_2 b_1 = a_1 + a_2 .$$

This last result indicates that the specified $a_1$, $b_1$, $a_2$, and $b_2$ must satisfy this relationship in order for there to exist a hyperbola with all of the specified properties.

Since the original equation defining the hyperbola was a homogeneous equation, any one of the parameters can be specified arbitrarily. Therefore, arbitrarily select

$$C = 1 .$$

To summarize, when using a hyperbola as the model for the utility function $U(p)$, the procedure is the following. Select $a_1$, $b_1$, $a_2$ and $b_2$, subject to the restrictions, $a_1 > 0$, $0 \leqslant b_1 < 1$, $a_2 > 0$, $b_2 > 1$, and $a_1 b_2 + a_2 b_1 = a_1 + a_2$. The corresponding hyperbola is defined by the equation,

$$b_1 b_2 p^2 - (b_1 + b_2)pU(p) + U^2(p) + (a_1 + a_2)p - (a_1 + a_2)U(p) = 0 .$$

Furthermore,

$$2U(p) = (b_1 + b_2)p + (a_1 + a_2) - Q,$$

$$2U^{(1)}(p) = (b_1 + b_2) - \frac{T}{Q},$$

$$2U^{(2)}(p) = \frac{\left(\dfrac{T}{Q}\right)^2 - 2(b_2 - b_1)^2}{Q},$$

$$U^{(3)}(p) = -3U^{(2)}(p)\left[\frac{T}{Q^2}\right],$$

where

$$Q = \sqrt{[(b_1 + b_2)p + (a_1 + a_2)]^2 - 4[b_1 b_2 p^2 + (a_1 + a_2)p]}$$

$$= \sqrt{[(b_2 - b_1)p + (a_1 + a_2)]^2 + 4(a_1 + a_2)(b_1 - 1)p}$$

and

$$T = (b_2 - b_1)^2 p + (a_1 + a_2)(b_1 + b_2 - 2).$$

Given $E\{P(\delta)\}$ and $\text{Var}\{P(\delta)\}$, these results permit computing an approximation of $E\{U(P(\delta))\}$ as outlined in Section 5.2.

## 5.4. An exponential model

This section will formulate a utility function model which is similar to the one in the preceding section. The basic differences are that it yields simpler results but it does not provide as much flexibility for fitting the curve as desired. The model assumes that $U(p)$ converges to an asymptote, $a_1 + b_1 x$ (where $a_1 > 0, 0 \leqslant b_1 < 1$), as $p$ increases (just as with the preceding model), but that $U(p)$ diverges from this asymptote exponentially as $p$ decreases. In other words, the assumed form of the function is

$$U(p) = a_1 + b_1 p - k_1 e^{-k_2 p}.$$

The convention that $U(p)$ passes through the origin with slope one completely determines $k_1$ and $k_2$. $U(0) = 0$ implies that

$$k_1 = a_1 .$$

$U'(0) = 1$ implies that $b_1 + k_1 k_2 = 1$, so that

$$k_2 = \frac{1-b_1}{a_1} .$$

Therefore, the desired utility function is

$$U(p) = a_1 + b_1 p - a_1 e^{-\left(\frac{1-b_1}{a_1}\right)p} .$$

Furthermore,

$$U^{(1)}(p) = b_1 + (1-b_1)e^{-\left(\frac{1-b_1}{a_1}\right)p} ;$$

$$U^{(2)}(p) = -a_1 \left(\frac{1-b_1}{a_1}\right)^2 e^{-\left(\frac{1-b_1}{a_1}\right)p} ;$$

$$U^{(3)}(p) = a_1 \left(\frac{1-b_1}{a_1}\right)^3 e^{-\left(\frac{1-b_1}{a_1}\right)p} .$$

Hence, if $E\{P(\delta)\}$ and $\mathrm{Var}\{P(\delta)\}$ are known, $E\{U(P(\delta))\}$ can be approximated with a minimum of effort by the method given in Section 5.2.

When $P(\delta)$ has a normal distribution, it is also possible to obtain an exact expression for $E\{U(P(\delta))\}$. Suppose that $P(\delta)$ is normal with mean $\mu$ and variance $\sigma^2$. MOOD (1950, p. 112) shows that the moment-generating function for such a normal random variable is

$$E\{e^{tP(\delta)}\} = e^{t\mu + (t^2\sigma^2/2)} .$$

Therefore,

$$E\{U(P(\delta))\} = E\{a_1 + b_1 P(\delta) - a_1 e^{-\left(\frac{1-b_1}{a_1}\right)P(\delta)}\}$$

$$= a_1 + b_1\mu - a_1 e^{-\left(\frac{1-b_1}{a_1}\right)\mu + \left(\frac{1-b_1}{a_1}\right)^2 \sigma^2/2} .$$

The hyperbola model and the exponential model share the virtue that they reduce the problem of subjectively estimating the utility function $U(p)$ to one of subjectively estimating the asymptote(s) of $U(p)$.

# CHAPTER 6

# APPROXIMATE AND EXACT SOLUTION PROCEDURES

## 6.1. Formulation

The preceding chapters have dealt with various aspects of the problem formulated in Section 1.6. The purpose of this chapter is to integrate these results into systematic procedures for efficiently obtaining suboptimal and optimal solutions to this problem. Thus, Section 6.2 develops an approximate procedure which is based on solving a sequence of linear programming problems. Given the resulting suboptimal solution, Section 6.4 then develops an exact procedure for continuing on to an optimal solution by means of a branch-and-bound algorithm presented in Section 6.3. However, the price that must be paid for obtaining the computational efficiency inherent in these procedures is that the formulation of the problem must be made a little less general than heretofore. The new assumptions required by both procedures, and the resulting simplifications in the model, are presented below. Additional assumptions required by only the exact procedure will be given in Section 6.4.

**Assumption 1:** The model of cash flows has the same form as that developed in Chapter 3.

It should be noted that Assumption 1 does not require that the model of cash flows contain all of the terms presented in Chapter 3, or that the interpretation of the terms must be the same as given there. What is required is that $X_j(\delta)$ must equal the sum of one or more of the following functions: (1) a linear combination of the $\delta_k$, where the coefficients are random variables or sums of random variables, (2) a deterministic function of $\delta$, and (3) a linear combination of random variables which are independent of those in (1), where the coefficients are themselves linear combinations of the $\delta_k$ with constant coefficients. For convenience, the notation introduced in Chapter 3 will continue to be used here.

**Assumption 2:** For each $j$ $(j = 1, ..., n)$, $i_j(\delta)$ equals the same constant, $i_j$, for all $\delta \in S$.

As a result of Assumptions 1 and 2, $P(\delta)$ may be expressed as

$$P(\delta) = \sum_{k=1}^{m} P_k \delta_k + h(\delta),$$

where

$$P_k = \sum_{j=1}^{n} \sum_{l=1}^{m_k} \left[ \frac{Y_{jkl}}{\prod\limits_{t=1}^{j} (1+i_t)} \right] + \sum_{j=1}^{n} \sum_{l=1}^{e} \left[ \frac{\sigma_{jkl} Z_{jl}}{\prod\limits_{t=1}^{j} (1+i_t)} \right], \text{ for } k = 1, ..., m,$$

$$h(\delta) = \sum_{j=1}^{n} \left[ \frac{h_j(\delta)}{\prod\limits_{t=1}^{j} (1+i_t)} \right],$$

so that the $P_k$ are random variables whose joint probability distribution is not disturbed by the choice of $\delta$.

**Assumption 3:** $h_1(\delta), ..., h_n(\delta)$, and therefore $h(\delta)$ are "pairwise additive", so that

$$h(\delta) = \sum_{j=1}^{m} \sum_{\substack{k=1 \\ k \neq j}}^{m} \mu_{jk} \delta_j \delta_k,$$

where the $\mu_{jk}$ are specified constants such that $\mu_{jk} = \mu_{kj}$ for all $k$ and $j$.

The interpretation of Assumption 3 is that, for each $\delta \in S$, either the only competitive or complementary effects are between pairs of investments or any joint effect involving more than two investments is merely the cumulation of the pairwise effects. Because of Assumption 3, $P(\delta)$ now reduces to

$$P(\delta) = \sum_{k=1}^{n} P_k \delta_k + \sum_{j=1}^{m} \sum_{\substack{k=1 \\ k \neq j}}^{m} \mu_{jk} \delta_j \delta_k .$$

Obtaining this expression was actually the reason for making Assumptions 1, 2, and 3, so any other route that arrives at this same point also would suffice.

**Assumption 4:** $U(p)$ has a finite 3rd derivative $U^{(3)}(p)$ for all $p$, and $U^{(2)}(p)$ is continuous everywhere.

Since Assumption 4 satisfies the hypotheses of Taylor's Theorem for $N = 3$, the results derived in Section 5.2 may be used. Thus, in particular,

$$E\{U(P(\delta))\} = U(\mu) + \frac{U^{(2)}(\mu)}{2} \sigma^2 + R ,$$

where $\mu = E\{P(\delta)\}$, $\sigma^2 = \mathrm{Var}\{P(\delta)\}$, and $R$ is the remainder term given there.

Fortunately, $E\{P(\delta)\}$ and $\mathrm{Var}\{P(\delta)\}$ now reduce to simple functions of $\delta$. Thus,

$$E\{P(\delta)\} = \sum_{k=1}^{m} \mu_k \delta_k + \sum_{j=1}^{m} \sum_{\substack{k=1 \\ k \neq j}}^{m} \mu_{jk} \delta_j \delta_k ,$$

where

$$\mu_k = E(P_k) = \sum_{j=1}^{n} \sum_{l=1}^{m_k} \frac{E(Y_{jkl})}{\prod_{t=1}^{j}(1+i_t)} + \sum_{j=1}^{m} \sum_{l=1}^{e} \frac{\sigma_{jkl} E(Z_{jl})}{\prod_{t=1}^{j}(1+i_t)} , \text{ for } k = 1, \ldots, m .$$

To obtain a similar expression for $\mathrm{Var}\{P(\delta)\}$, note that

$$\text{Var}\{P(\boldsymbol{\delta})\} = \text{Var}\left\{\sum_{k=1}^{m} P_k \delta_k\right\}$$

$$= \sum_{j_1=1}^{n} \sum_{k_1=1}^{m} \sum_{l_1=1}^{m_{k_1}} \sum_{j_2=1}^{n} \sum_{k_2=1}^{m} \sum_{l_2=1}^{m_{k_2}} \left[ \frac{\text{Cov}\{Y_{j_1 k_1 l_1}, Y_{j_2 k_2 l_2}\}}{\prod_{t=1}^{j_1}(1+i_t) \prod_{t=1}^{j_2}(1+i_t)} \right] \delta_{k_1} \delta_{k_2}$$

$$+ \sum_{j_1=1}^{n} \sum_{l_1=1}^{e} \sum_{j_2=1}^{n} \sum_{l_2=1}^{e} \left[ \left( \sum_{k_1=1}^{m} \frac{\sigma_{j_1 k_1 l_1}}{\prod_{t=1}^{j_1}(1+i_t)} \delta_{k_1} \right) \left( \sum_{k_2=1}^{m} \frac{\sigma_{j_2 k_2 l_2}}{\prod_{t=1}^{j_2}(1+i_t)} \delta_{k_2} \right) \right.$$

$$\left. \vphantom{\sum} \text{Cov}\{Z_{j_1 l_1}, Z_{j_2 l_2}\} \right] .$$

(There are no covariance terms involving both $Y_{jkl}$ and $Z_{jl}$, since the $Z_{jl}$ are functions of exogenous variables and therefore statistically independent of the $Y_{jkl}$.) Therefore, by combining the coefficients of $\delta_{k_1} \delta_{k_2}$, and noting that $\delta_k = \delta_k^2$, it now follows that

$$\text{Var}\{P(\boldsymbol{\delta})\} = \sum_{k=1}^{m} \sigma_k^2 \delta_k + \sum_{j=1}^{m} \sum_{\substack{k=1 \\ k \neq j}}^{m} \sigma_{jk} \delta_j \delta_k ,$$

where

$$\sigma_{jk} = \sum_{j_1=1}^{n} \sum_{j_2=1}^{n}$$

$$\left[ \frac{\sum_{l_1=1}^{m_j} \sum_{l_2=1}^{m_k} \text{Cov}\{Y_{j_1 j l_1}, Y_{j_2 k l_2}\} + \sum_{l_1=1}^{e} \sum_{l_2=1}^{e} \sigma_{j_1 j l_1} \sigma_{j_2 k l_2} \text{Cov}\{Z_{j_1 l_1}, Z_{j_2 l_2}\}}{\prod_{t=1}^{j_1}(1+i_t) \prod_{t=1}^{j_2}(1+i_t)} \right],$$

$$\text{for } j = 1, ..., m; \ k = 1, ..., m,$$

$$\sigma_k^2 = \sigma_{kk}, \quad \text{for} \quad k = 1, ..., m .$$

(Note that $\sigma_{jk}=\sigma_{kj}$ for all $j$ and $k$.) Hence, except for the $R$ term, $E\{U(P(\delta))\}$ is now seen to depend on $\delta$ in a relatively simple way. Since the objective is to maximize $E\{U(P(\delta))\}$ over $\delta \in S$, this will prove to be very useful for developing the solution procedures in the following sections.

## 6.2. An approximate linear programming approach

WEINGARTNER (1963) has thoroughly studied how to solve the capital budgeting problem under certainty by a linear programming approach. Unfortunately, this approach cannot be extended in an exact way to the problem being considered here, since both the introduction of risk (with the resulting expected utility criterion) and the consideration of competitive and complementary effects make the objective function non-linear. However, by introducing suitable linear approximations, and by solving a sequence of linear programming problems rather than one, the same basic approach may be used to obtain a good suboptimal solution. This is outlined below.

The general structure of the linear programming model to be used here is

$$\text{maximize} \quad \sum_{j=1}^{m} c_j \delta_j ,$$

$$\text{subject to} \quad \delta \in S ,$$

where the $c_j$ are constants to be specified. Weingartner has shown how to express the basic capital budgeting constraints in a linear programming format (see Section 1.5 and its footnote), and it is assumed here that $\delta \in S$ can be expressed in this way. The one exception is that the requirement that $\delta_j=0$ or $1$ $(j = 1, ..., m)$ is replaced (at least at the outset) by the constraint, $0 \leqslant \delta_j \leqslant 1$ $(j = 1, ..., m)$.

The objective of the first series of steps is to find a $\delta$ that approximately maximizes $E\{P(\delta)\}$ over $\delta \in S$. It will be seen that this preliminary solution permits obtaining a good linear approximation of $E\{U(P(\delta))\}$, which can then be used to obtain the final solution.

**Step 1:** Set $c_j = \mu_j$ for $j = 1, ..., m$, and solve the resulting linear programming problem by the simplex method. Denote the resulting solution by $\delta^{(1)} = (\delta_1^{(1)}, ..., \delta_m^{(1)})$.

**Step 2:** Reset $c_j = \mu_j + 2 \sum_{\substack{k=1 \\ k \neq j}}^{m} \mu_{jk} \delta_k^{(1)}$ for $j = 1, ..., m$, and solve the resulting linear programming problem beginning from $\delta^{(1)}$. This value of $c_j$ is obtained from the expression for $E\{P(\delta)\}$ given in Section 6.1. The summation term is multiplied by two in order to approximate the correct marginal effect of changing $\delta_j$, since it is this marginal effect rather than the magnitude of the objective function that is relevant for decision making. Denote the resulting solution by $\delta^{(2)} = (\sigma_1^{(2)}, ..., \delta_m^{(2)})$.

**Step 3:** Reset $c_j = \mu_j + 2 \sum_{\substack{k=1 \\ k \neq j}}^{m} \mu_{jk} \delta_k^{(2)}$ for $j = 1, ..., m$. There are then two alternative ways to proceed in order to obtain the desired feasible integer solution that approximately maximizes $E\{P(\delta)\}$ over $\delta \in S$. One way is to solve the resulting linear programming problem (beginning from $\delta^{(2)}$) and then attempt to round the fractional variables up or down in such a way as to obtain a feasible integer solution while maintaining a relatively large value of $E\{P(\delta)\}$. Fortunately, according to a theorem due to WEINGARTNER (1963, pp. 35 ff.), the number of fractional variables in this linear programming solution cannot exceed the number of functional constraints. Since capital budgeting problems often have only a small number of such constraints, there may only be a few variables that will need adjusting. Alternatively, one can immediately impose the restriction that the $\delta_j$ must be integer, and then apply one of the available algorithms for the resulting pure integer linear programming problem. These include the optimal algorithms developed by GOMORY (1958b, 1960) and others that have been surveyed by BALINSKY (1965) and BEALE (1965), plus some more recent ones developed by BALAS (1965), GLOVER (1965), and the author (HILLIER 1966b). However, since these algorithms tend to be relatively inefficient, and only a suboptimal solution is being sought anyway, it is probably preferable to use an efficient suboptimal algorithm such as those developed by the author (HILLIER 1966a).

Whichever method is used in Step 3, let $\delta^{(3)} = (\delta_1^{(3)}, \ldots, \delta_m^{(3)})$ be the resulting solution, and let $\mu^{(3)} = E\{P(\delta^{(3)})\}$. It is anticipated that the value of $E\{P(\delta)\}$ for the interesting values of $\delta$ should be of the same order of magnitude as $\mu^{(3)}$. Therefore, if $U^{(2)}(\mu)$ is close to zero for $\mu$ relatively close to $\mu^{(3)}$, then $U(\mu^{(3)}) + U^{(1)}(\mu^{(3)})(\mu - \mu^{(3)})$ should be a reasonable approximation of $U(\mu)$ for such $\mu$. Similarly, $U^{(2)}(\mu)$ should be close to $U^{(2)}(\mu^{(3)})$ for the interesting values of $\mu$. Further assume that the remainder term $R$ is either close to zero or close to some other constant value for all interesting $\delta \in S$, so that it can be safely ignored for decision making purposes. Under these conditions,

$$E\{U(P(\delta))\} \doteq U(\mu^{(3)}) + U^{(1)}(\mu^{(3)})(\mu - \mu^{(3)}) + \frac{U^{(2)}(\mu^{(3)})}{2}\sigma^2$$

should be a good approximation for relevant $\delta$. Therefore, the variable portion of $E\{U(P(\delta))\}$ would be

$$U^{(1)}(\mu^{(3)})\mu + \frac{U^{(2)}(\mu^{(3)})}{2}\sigma^2 = U^{(1)}(\mu^{(3)}) \left[ \sum_{j=1}^{m} \mu_j \delta_j + \sum_{j=1}^{m} \sum_{\substack{k=1 \\ k \neq j}}^{m} \mu_{jk} \delta_j \delta_k \right]$$

$$+ \frac{U^{(2)}(\mu^{(3)})}{2} \left[ \sum_{j=1}^{m} \sigma_j^2 \delta_j + \sum_{j=1}^{m} \sum_{\substack{k=1 \\ k \neq j}}^{m} \sigma_{jk} \delta_j \delta_k \right].$$

Recall that $\mu_{jk} = \mu_{kj}$ and $\sigma_{jk} = \sigma_{kj}$ for all $j$ and $k$. Hence, if $\delta_j$ were allowed to be a continuous variable, then

$$\frac{\partial E\{U(P(\delta))\}}{\partial \delta_j} \Bigg|_{\delta = \delta^{(3)}} \doteq U^{(1)}(\mu^{(3)}) \left[ \mu_j + 2 \sum_{\substack{k=1 \\ k \neq j}}^{m} \mu_{jk} \delta_k^{(3)} \right]$$

$$+ \frac{U^{(2)}(\mu^{(3)})}{2} \left[ \sigma_j^2 + 2 \sum_{\substack{k=1 \\ k \neq j}}^{m} \sigma_{jk} \delta_k^{(3)} \right].$$

This approximation of the marginal effect of changing $\delta_j$ is the key result that will now permit finding a $\delta$ that approximately maximizes $E\{U(P(\delta))\}$ over $\delta \in S$, as shown below.

**Step 4:** Reset $c_j = U^{(1)}(\mu^{(3)}) \left[ \mu_j + 2 \sum_{\substack{k=1 \\ k \neq j}}^{m} \mu_{jk} \delta_k^{(3)} \right]$

$$+ \frac{U^{(2)}(\mu^{(3)})}{2} \left[ \sigma_j^2 + 2 \sum_{\substack{k=1 \\ k \neq j}}^{m} \sigma_{jk} \delta_k^{(3)} \right]$$

for $j = 1, \ldots, m$, and solve the resulting linear programming problem beginning from the last basic feasible solution obtained above. Denote the resulting solution by $\delta^{(4)} = (\delta_1^{(4)}, \ldots, \delta_m^{(4)})$, and let $\mu^{(4)} = E\{P(\delta^{(4)})\}$.

**Step 5:** Reset $c_j = U^{(1)}(\mu^{(4)}) \left[ \mu_j + 2 \sum_{\substack{k=1 \\ k \neq j}}^{m} \mu_{jk} \delta_k^{(4)} \right]$

$$+ \frac{U^{(2)}(\mu^{(4)})}{2} \left[ \sigma_j^2 + 2 \sum_{\substack{k=1 \\ k \neq j}}^{m} \sigma_{jk} \delta_k^{(4)} \right]$$

for $j = 1, \ldots, m$, and then proceed by either of the two alternative solution procedures described in Step 3. This yields the desired solution that approximately maximizes $E\{U(P(\delta))\}$ over $\delta \in S$.

Although the above 5-step procedure will not necessarily find an optimal solution, it is of considerable interest for several reasons. One is that the exact solution procedure developed in the next two sections is considerably expedited if preliminary solutions for $\mu$ and $\delta$ are first obtained from Steps 3 and 5, respectively. Another reason is the convenience and relatively high computational efficiency associated with the approximate procedure. It only needs to use linear programming solution procedures, for which computer codes are widely available and highly efficient. Even choosing the option of using suboptimal integer linear programming algorithms in Steps 3 and 5 would be highly efficient. Furthermore, the ordinary linear programming calculations automatically provide the corresponding dual solution. As WEINGARTNER (1963) has discussed, the dual evaluators play a very important role in analyzing capital budgeting problems.

Finally, perhaps the most critical reason for introducing this approximate linear programming approach is the ease with which sensitivity analysis can be conducted by standard linear programming techniques and duality theory (e.g., see HILLIER and LIEBERMAN 1967b). It has been taken for granted thus far that such input data as the parameters of the utility function model, the $i_j$, etc., can be specified precisely. This of course is not usually the case in practice. Therefore, it may be important to do extensive experimentation with alternative values for the input parameters. The final decision on $\delta$ might then be made by management on the basis of this sensitivity analysis. This kind of approach is easily implemented within the context of this approximate procedure.

## 6.3. A relevant branch-and-bound algorithm

This section presents a branch-and-bound algorithm which will form the basis of the exact solution procedure summarized in Section 6.4. Since this algorithm will be applied to two different parts of the problem under consideration, it is presented here within the context of a certain general type of mathematical programming problem.

Branch-and-bound algorithms have become popular in recent years as a relatively efficient truncated enumeration method for solving difficult combinatorial problems. For example, LITTLE *et al.* (1963) applied this approach with considerable success to the traveling salesman problem, and several investigators have developed versions of it for the integer linear programming problem. It also seems to be a natural approach to solving the problem formulated in Section 6.1.

The branch-and-bound algorithm developed here is applicable to the general problem of choosing the $m$-vector, $\varDelta = (\varDelta_1, ..., \varDelta_m)$, so as to

$$\max f(\varDelta),$$

$$\text{subject to } \varDelta \in F,$$

where the set $F \subset \{\varDelta | \varDelta_j = 0 \text{ or } 1; j = 1, ..., m\}$, and where the following conditions hold. There exists a known function $g(\varDelta)$ such that

$$g(\varDelta) = a + \sum_{j=1}^{m} b_j \varDelta_j + \sum_{j=1}^{m} \sum_{\substack{k=1 \\ k \neq j}}^{m} c_{jk} \varDelta_j \varDelta_k \, ,$$

where the $b_j, c_{jk}$, and $a$ are given constants, and

$$g(\varDelta) \geqslant f(\varDelta) \quad \text{for all} \quad \varDelta \in F \, .$$

Also given are a suboptimal solution $\varDelta^*$ such that $f(\varDelta^*)$ is close to $\max_{\varDelta \in F} f(\varDelta)$ and a tractable method of calculating $f(\varDelta)$ for any given $\varDelta \in F$.

The objective is to have an automatic solution procedure that can be executed on a digital computer, where this procedure would be much more efficient than exhaustive enumeration when $[g(\varDelta) - f(\varDelta)]$ is small for most $\varDelta \in F$.

Certain notation required by the algorithm will now be introduced. Given a partial solution for $\varDelta$, i.e., a specification of values for certain components of $\varDelta$, let

$$J_0 = \{j | \varDelta_j = 0\} \, ,$$
$$J_1 = \{j | \varDelta_j = 1\} \, ,$$
$$J_N = \{j | \text{no value assigned to } \varDelta_j\} \, .$$

Given $J_0$, $J_1$, and $J_N$, let

$$P = (\varDelta | \varDelta_j = 0 \quad \text{if} \quad j \in J_0, \qquad \varDelta_j = 1 \quad \text{if} \quad j \in J_1\} \, ,$$

$$B_j(J_0, J_1, J_N) = b_j + \sum_{\substack{k \in J_1 \\ k \neq j}} c_{jk} + \sum_{\substack{k \in J_N \\ k \neq j}} \max \{c_{jk}, 0\}, \quad \text{for} \quad j = 1, \dots, m \, ,$$

$$B(J_0, J_1, J_N) = a + \sum_{j \in J_1} B_j(J_0, J_1, J_N) + \sum_{j \in J_N} \max \{B_j(J_0, J_1, J_N), 0\} \, .$$

Thus,

$$B(J_0, J_1, J_N) \geqslant g(\varDelta) \quad \text{for all} \quad \varDelta \in P \, ,$$

where $P$ is the set of completions for the given partial solution. (A completion of a partial solution is a specification of the other components of $\varDelta$ not included in the partial solution.) Therefore,

$$B(J_0, J_1, J_N) \geqslant f(\varDelta) \quad \text{for all} \quad \varDelta \in P \cap F \, ,$$

so that $P$ can be eliminated from further consideration if $B(J_0, J_1, J_N)$ is less than some known lower bound on $\max\limits_{\Delta \in F} f(\Delta)$. This fact plays a key role in the algorithm.

The basic idea of the algorithm is the following. The components of $\Delta$ are first reordered in a convenient way, where partial solutions would be constructed by assigning values to the components in this order. The value of $f(\Delta)$ for the best feasible solution that is currently known is used as a lower bound on $\max\limits_{\Delta \in F} f(\Delta)$. Given the partial solution for the current iteration, the next partial solution is obtained by making one of the three following decisions: (1) eliminate $P$ from further consideration, releasing the last specified component of $\Delta$, or (2) assign a value of zero to the next unspecified component of $\Delta$, or (3) assign a value of one to this component. The choice between these decisions is based on which of the following quantities is largest: (1) the lower bound on $\max\limits_{\Delta \in F} f(\Delta)$, or (2) the value of $B(J_0, J_1, J_N)$ that would result from the second decision, or (3) the value of $B(J_0, J_1, J_N)$ that would result from the third decision. A new best known feasible solution is obtained when all of the components of $\Delta$ have been specified, after which decision (1) is then made. The algorithm terminates when all possible solutions have been eliminated from further consideration, at which point the best known feasible solution is identified as an optimal solution.

To avoid reconsidering $\Delta_j$ needlessly, any $\Delta_j$ that definitely should be set at a particular value should be assigned this value permanently at the outset. To implement this, let $e^{(j)}$ be the unit $m$-vector such that component $j$ equals one and all other components equal zero ($j=1, ..., m$), and let

$$Q^{(j)} = \{\Delta | \Delta_j = 1, \quad \Delta \in F, \quad [\Delta - e^{(j)}] \in F\},$$

$$Q_1^{(j)} = \{\Delta | \Delta_j = 1, \quad \Delta \in F, \quad [\Delta - e^{(j)}] \notin F\},$$

$$Q_0^{(j)} = \{\Delta | \Delta_j = 0, \quad \Delta \in F, \quad [\Delta + e^{(j)}] \notin F\}.$$

Then $j$ will be said to be "ineligible" for assignment to $J_1$ if

$$f(\Delta) \leqslant f(\Delta - e^{(j)}) \quad \text{for all} \quad \Delta \in Q^{(j)}$$

and

$$f(\Delta) < \max_{\Delta \in F} f(\Delta) \quad \text{for all} \quad \Delta \in Q_1^{(j)}.$$

The latter condition usually would be very difficult to verify unless $Q_1^{(j)} = \varphi$, in which case it is satisfied trivially. (Therefore, it normally would not be worthwhile trying to check if $j$ is ineligible if $Q_1^{(j)} \neq \varphi$.) Similarly, $j$ will be said to be "ineligible" for assignment to $J_0$ if

$$f(\Delta - e^{(j)}) \leqslant f(\Delta) \quad \text{for all} \quad \Delta \in Q^{(j)}$$

and

$$f(\Delta) < \max_{\Delta \in F} f(\Delta) \quad \text{for all} \quad \Delta \in Q_0^{(j)}.$$

The main computational task in the algorithm is calculating the two new values of $B(J_0, J_1, J_N)$ at each iteration. A lemma is given below that indicates how this can be done more efficiently than by completely recalculating $B(J_0, J_1, J_N)$ each time. Following the proof of the lemma, an algebraic summary of the algorithm will be presented.

**Lemma:** If $k^* \in J_N$, then

$$B(J_0, J_1 \cup \{k^*\}, J_N - \{k^*\}) = \tfrac{1}{2}(s + d),$$
$$B(J_0 \cup \{k^*\}, J_1, J_N - \{k^*\}) = \tfrac{1}{2}(s - d),$$

where

$$s = 2B(J_0, J_1, J_N) - |B_{k^*}(J_0, J_1, J_N)| - \sum_{j \in J_1} |c_{jk^*}| - \sum_{\substack{j \in J_N \\ j \neq k^*}} |w_j|$$

$$d = B_{k^*}(J_0, J_1, J_N) + \sum_{j \in J_1} c_{jk^*} + \sum_{\substack{j \in J_N \\ j \neq k^*}} w_j,$$

where, for each $j \in J_N - \{k^*\}$,

$$w_j = \begin{cases} c_{jk^*}, & \text{if } |c_{jk^*}| \leqslant \max\{B_j(J_0, J_1, J_N), 0\} \\ \max\{B_j(J_0, J_1, J_N), 0\}, & \text{if } c_{jk^*} \geqslant \max\{B_j(J_0, J_1, J_N), 0\} \\ -\max\{B_j(J_0, J_1, J_N), 0\}, & \text{if } c_{jk^*} \leqslant -\max\{B_j(J_0, J_1, J_N), 0\}. \end{cases}$$

**Proof:** Note that

$$B(J_0, J_1 \cup \{k^*\}, J_N - \{k^*\}) = B(J_0, J_1, J_N) + \min\{B_{k^*}(J_0, J_1, J_N), \ 0\}$$
$$+ \sum_{j \in J_1} \min\{c_{jk^*}, 0\} + \sum_{\substack{j \in J_N \\ j \neq k^*}} \max\{-\max\{B_j(J_0, J_1, J_N), \ 0\}, \ \min\{c_{jk^*}, 0\}\},$$

and

$$B(J_0 \cup \{k^*\}, J_1, J_N - \{k^*\}) = B(J_0, J_1, J_N) - \max\{B_{k^*}(J_0, J_1, J_N), \ 0\}$$
$$- \sum_{j \in J_1} \max\{c_{jk^*}, 0\} - \sum_{\substack{j \in J_N \\ j \neq k^*}} \min\{\max\{B_j(J_0, J_1, J_N), \ 0\}, \max\{c_{jk}, \ 0\}\}.$$

Setting

$$s = B(J_0, J_1 \cup \{k^*\}, \ J_N - \{k^*\}) + B(J_0 \cup \{k^*\}, \ J_1, J_N - \{k^*\}),$$
$$d = B(J_0, J_1 \cup \{k^*\}, \ J_N - \{k^*\}) - B(J_0 \cup \{k^*\}, \ J_1, J_N - \{k^*\}),$$

then yields the desired result.

### Summary of algorithm

**Step 1:** Set $J_0 = \varphi, J_1 = \varphi, J_N = \{1, \ldots, m\}, \varDelta^* = \varDelta^*, f^* = f(\varDelta^*)$.

**Step 2:** Set $\varDelta_j = 0$ and transfer $j$ from $J_N$ to $J_0$ for each $j \in J_N$ that is known to be ineligible for assignment to $J_1$ (see preceding discussion). Set $\varDelta_j = 1$ and transfer $j$ from $J_N$ to $J_1$ for each $j \in J_N$ that is known to be ineligible for assignment to $J_0$. Repeat as necessary if this has made additional values of $j$ ineligible. (Let $m'$ be the number of elements remaining in $J_N$.)

**Step 3:** Set $B_j = b_j + \sum_{\substack{k \in J_1 \\ k \neq j}} c_{jk} + \sum_{\substack{k \in J_N \\ k \neq j}} \max\{c_{jk}, 0\}$ for each $j \in J_1 \cup J_N$ and set

$$B^{(0)} = a + \sum_{j \in J_1} B_j + \sum_{j \in J_N} \max\{B_j, \ 0\}.$$

**Step 4:** Set $(k_1, k_2, \ldots, k_{m'})$ equal to a permutation of the elements of $J_N$ such that $B_{k_1} \geqslant \ldots \geqslant B_{k_{m'}}$. Set $J = J_N$ and $t = 1$.

**Step 5:** Set

$$
w_j = \begin{cases}
c_{jk_t}, & \text{if } \ |c_{jk_t}| \leq \quad \max\{B_j, 0\} \\
\max\{B_j, 0\}, & \text{if } \ c_{jk_t} > \quad \max\{B_j, 0\} \\
-\max\{B_j, 0\}, & \text{if } \ c_{jk_t} < -\max\{B_j, 0\}
\end{cases}
$$

for each $j \in J_N - \{k_t\}$. Then set

$$
s = 2B^{(t-1)} - |B_{k_t}| - \sum_{j \in J_1} |c_{jk_t}| - \sum_{\substack{j \in J_N \\ j \neq k_t}} |w_j|,
$$

$$
d = B_{k_t} + \sum_{j \in J_1} c_{jk_t} + \sum_{\substack{j \in J_N \\ j \neq k_t}} w_j.
$$

Then set

$$
B^{(t)}(1) = \tfrac{1}{2}(s+d),
$$
$$
B^{(t)}(0) = \tfrac{1}{2}(s-d).
$$

**Step 6:** Check if $P \cap F = \varphi$ if $k_t$ were to be transferred from $J_N$ to $J_1$ (i.e., check if $\Delta_{k_t} = 1$ would be an "infeasible branch"); if so, then reset $B^{(t)}(1) = -\infty$. Then check if $P \cap F = \varphi$ if $k_t$ were to be transferred from $J_N$ to $J_0$ instead; if so, then reset $B^{(t)}(0) = -\infty$. (See the preceding discussion for the definitions of $P$ and $F$.)

**Step 7:** Check if $\max\{B^{(t)}(1), B^{(t)}(0)\} > f^*$.
(a) If $\max\{B^{(t)}(1), B^{(t)}(0)\} > f^*$, then go to Step 8.
(b) If $\max\{B^{(t)}(1), B^{(t)}(0)\} \leq f^*$, then go to Step 13.

**Step 8:** Check if $B^{(t)}(1) > B^{(t)}(0)$.
(a) If $B^{(t)}(1) > B^{(t)}(0)$, then set $\Delta_{k_t} = 1$, transfer $k_t$ from $J_N$ to $J_1$, set $B^{(t)} = B^{(t)}(1)$, and reset $B_j = B_j + \min\{c_{jk_t}, 0\}$ for each $j \in J - \{k_t\}$; then go to Step 9.
(b) If $B^{(t)}(1) \leq B^{(t)}(0)$, then set $\Delta_{k_t} = 0$, transfer $k_t$ from $J_N$ to $J_0$, set $B^{(t)} = B^{(t)}(0)$, and reset $B_j = B_j - \max\{c_{jk_t}, 0\}$ for each $j \in J - \{k_t\}$; then go to Step 12.

**Step 9:** Set

$$\Delta_j^{(0)} = \begin{cases} 1, & \text{if } j \in J_1 \\ 0, & \text{otherwise}, \end{cases}$$

and then check if $\Delta^{(0)} \in F$.
(a) If $\Delta^{(0)} \in F$, then set $f^{(0)} = f(\Delta^{(0)})$ and go to Step 10.
(b) If $\Delta^{(0)} \notin F$, then go to Step 12.

**Step 10:** Check if $f^{(0)} > f^*$.
(a) If $f^{(0)} > f^*$, then reset $f^* = f^{(0)}$, $\Delta^* = \Delta^{(0)}$, and go to Step 11.
(b) If $f^{(0)} \leqslant f^*$, then go to Step 12.

**Step 11:** Check if $B^{(t)} > f^*$.
(a) If $B^{(t)} > f^*$, then go to Step 12.
(b) If $B^{(t)} \leqslant f^*$, then go to Step 15.

**Step 12:** Check if $t < m'$.
(a) If $t < m'$, then reset $t = t+1$ and go to Step 5.
(b) If $t = m'$, then go to Step 14.

**Step 13:** Check if $t > 1$.
(a) If $t > 1$, then reset $t = t-1$ and go to Step 15.
(b) If $t = 1$, then $\Delta^*$ is an optimal solution and the algorithm is terminated.

**Step 14:** Check if $f(\Delta) > f^*$.
(a) If $f(\Delta) > f^*$, then reset $f^* = f(\Delta)$, $\Delta^* = \Delta$, and go to Step 15.
(b) If $f(\Delta) \leqslant f^*$, then go to Step 15.

**Step 15:** Check $\Delta_{k_t}$.
(a) If $\Delta_{k_t} = 1$, then transfer $k_t$ from $J_1$ to $J_N$, reset $B^{(t)}(1) = -\infty$, and reset $B_j = B_j - \min\{c_{jk_t}, 0\}$ for each $j \in J - \{k_t\}$; then go to Step 7.
(b) If $\Delta_{k_t} = 0$, then transfer $k_t$ from $J_0$ to $J_N$, reset $B^{(t)}(0) = -\infty$, and reset $B_j = B_j + \max\{c_{jk_t}, 0\}$ for each $j \in J - \{k_t\}$; then go to Step 7.

**Justification of algorithm**

There are only three possible ways in which the completions of a particular partial solution can be eliminated from further consideration. The first is by Step 2, which cannot eliminate all optimal solutions. The second is by Step 6, in which case none of the completions is feasible. The third is by Step 15, which is executed only if the initial value of $B^{(t)}(\Delta_{k_t})$, which is an upper bound on $f(\Delta)$ for these completions, is less than or equal to $f(\Delta^*)$. Therefore, until $\Delta^*$ itself becomes an optimal solution in either Step 10 or Step 14, it is impossible to eliminate all other optimal solutions from consideration. Furthermore, the algorithm terminates only after all relevant solutions have been considered, so it necessarily finds an optimal solution. Finally, note that resetting $B^{(t)}(\Delta_{k_t}) = -\infty$ in Steps 6 and 15 prevents any partial solution from being considered more than once. The total number of relevant partial solutions is of course finite. Therefore, the algorithm must terminate with an optimal solution after a finite number of iterations.

Several possibilities for accelerating the algorithm will be discussed in the next section within the context of its application to the problem formulated in Section 6.1.

## 6.4. An exact solution procedure

The procedure given here involves solving two separate subproblems. The first and easier subproblem is to maximize $E\{P(\delta)$ over $\delta \in S$. Given the resulting solution, the procedure then maximizes $E\{U(P(\delta))\}$ over $\delta \in S$. Each subproblem will be discussed below in turn.

It was found in Section 6.1 that

$$E\{P(\delta)\} = \sum_{k=1}^{m} \mu_k \delta_k + \sum_{j=1}^{m} \sum_{\substack{k=1 \\ k \neq j}}^{m} \mu_{jk} \delta_j \delta_k .$$

Since this is a simple quadratic function, there are a number of possibilities for maximizing it over $\delta \in S$ under special circumstances. In particular, if $S = \{\delta | \delta_j = 0 \text{ or } 1; j = 1, ..., m\}$, so that all possible combinations of investments are feasible, then an algorithm developed by REITER (1963) is applicable. WEINGARTNER (1966, pp. 494–498) also discusses how to apply this algorithm when certain types of constraints are introduced. If $\delta \in S$ can be expressed in a linear programming format, and if rounding the fractional variables in a non-integer solution is adequate, then a non-concave quadratic programming algorithm developed by CANDLER and TOWNSLEY (1964) could be used. If, in addition, the objective function is concave (i.e., if the $m \times m$ matrix with zero diagonal elements and $\mu_{jk}$ as the element in row $j$, column $k$ ($j, k = 1, \ldots, m; j \neq k$) is negative semi-definite), then a considerable number of quadratic programming algorithms are available (e.g., see WOLFE 1959). If this matrix is actually negative definite, then an integer solution can be obtained in principle by integer quadratic programming algorithms developed by BOOT and THEIL (1963) and by KUNZI and OETTLI (1963).

However, a procedure that is well-suited for solving this subproblem in general is the algorithm presented in the preceding section. Merely let $\Delta = \delta$, set

$$f(\Delta) = \sum_{j=1}^{m} \mu_j \Delta_j + \sum_{j=1}^{m} \sum_{\substack{k=1 \\ k \neq j}}^{m} \mu_{jk} \Delta_j \Delta_k \,,$$

$$g(\Delta) \equiv f(\Delta) \,,$$

$$F = S \,,$$

and then apply this algorithm. Since $g(\Delta)$ is identical to rather than an upper bound on $f(\Delta)$, it should terminate relatively rapidly. Furthermore, if $Q_1^{(j)} = \varphi$, then it is easy to determine in Step 2 whether $j$ must be ineligible for assignment to $J_1$, since a sufficient condition is that

$$\mu_j + 2 \sum_{k \in J_1} \mu_{jk} + 2 \sum_{\substack{k \in J_N \\ k \neq j}} \max\{\mu_{jk}, 0\} \leqslant 0 \,.$$

Similarly, if $Q_0^{(j)} = \varphi$, then a sufficient condition for $j$ to be ineligible for assignment to $J_0$ in Step 2 is that

$$-\mu_j - 2 \sum_{k \in J_1} \mu_{jk} - 2 \sum_{\substack{k \in J_N \\ k \neq j}} \min\{\mu_{jk}, 0\} \leqslant 0 \,.$$

Let $\delta^*$ be the resulting optimal solution for the first subproblem, and let $\mu^* = E\{P(\delta^*)\}$ and $\sigma_*^2 = \text{Var}\{P(\delta^*)\}$. Then let $S^*$ be the subset of $S$ which excludes the solutions that do not satisfy the necessary conditions for optimality selected from Chapter 2.

Given $\delta^*$, a solution to the second subproblem can be obtained relatively efficiently in a somewhat similar way. However, the two additional assumptions given below need to be made in order to guarantee that this solution actually is optimal. (The adjustments required if they do not hold will be discussed briefly at the end of the section.)

**Assumption 5:** $E\{U(P(\delta))\} \leqslant U(\mu) + \dfrac{U^{(2)}(\mu)}{2}\sigma^2$ for all $\delta \in S^*$.

This assumption is of course equivalent to assuming that the remainder term $R$ given in Section 5.2 is non-negative for all $\delta \in S^*$. However, stated in this form, the assumption would tend to be difficult to verify. Fortunately, it is sufficient to verify the following set of conditions, which have a more meaningful interpretation.

**A sufficient set of conditions for assumption 5 to hold:**

(1) $U(p)$ has a finite $N$th derivative $U^{(N)}(p)$ for all $p$, and $U^{(N-1)}(p)$ is continuous everywhere, for $N = 4, 5, \ldots$.

(2) $U^{(k)}(\mu) \geqslant 0$ for $k = 3, 5, 7, \ldots$, and $U^{(k)}(\mu) \leqslant 0$ for $k = 4, 6, 8, \ldots$, for all $\mu$ such that $\mu = E\{P(\delta)\}$ for some $\delta \in S^*$.

(3) $E\{(P(\delta) - E\{P(\delta)\})^k\} \leqslant 0$ for $k = 3, 5, 7, \ldots$, for all $\delta \in S^*$.

It is readily seen that these conditions actually are sufficient by referring to the corresponding expression for $E\{U(P(\delta))\}$ given in Section 5.2. In fact, it is apparent that they tend to be considerably stronger than they need to be. Nevertheless, they are more likely to hold for practical problems than may be apparent at first glance. The first condition, which is essentially a mathematical convenience, holds for a wide class of utility functions, including those given in Sections 5.3 and 5.4. The second condition describes a utility function $U(p)$ that probably is concave and approaches an asymptote as $p$ increases. In particular, this condition is always satisfied for all possible values of $\mu$ by the exponential class of utility functions given in Section 5.4. Although it is not satisfied in general by the hyperbola model of Section 5.3, it does tend to hold for these utility functions also for the relevant case where the values of $\mu$ are somewhat above zero. The third condition merely implies that the probability distribution of $P(\delta)$ is either symmetrical, such as for the normal distribution, or skewed to the left. (See Section 4.2 for a discussion of the conditions under which the distribution of $P(\delta)$ is at least approximately normal.) Since risky investments by definition tend to have some probability of a sizable loss, it appears that this condition should be satisfied for most practical problems. Therefore, in summary, Assumption 5 definitely will be satisfied by any exponential utility function and most probability distributions of interest (including the normal distribution, any Beta distribution skewed to the left, etc.), and it probably will still hold if the utility function belongs to the hyperbola class (or something related) instead or even if the probability distribution is skewed slightly to the right.

**Assumption 6:** $U^{(1)}(p) \geqslant 0$, $U^{(2)}(p) \leqslant 0$, and $U^{(3)}(p) \geqslant 0$ for all $p$ such that $\min_{\delta \in S^*} E\{P(\delta)\} \leqslant p \leqslant \max_{\delta \in S^*} E\{P(\delta)\}$ .

This assumption merely says that, over the specified interval, $U(p)$ is a monotonic increasing concave function such that the rate at which the slope of $U(p)$ changes is decreasing as $p$ increases. These conditions should be satisfied by most utility functions of interest. They are always satisfied by the exponential model of Section 5.4. Utility functions belonging to the hyperbola class of Section 5.3 are always monotonic increasing and concave, and there always exists a number $p^*$ such that $U^{(3)}(p) \geqslant 0$ if $p \geqslant p^*$; thus, the only question is whether $p^* \leqslant \min_{\delta \in S^*} E\{P(\delta)\}$, and it appears that it usually should be.

It immediately follows from Assumptions 5 and 6 that, for each $\delta \in S^*$,

$$E\{U(P(\delta))\} \leqslant U(\mu^*) + U^{(1)}(\mu^*)(\mu - \mu^*) + \frac{U^{(2)}(\mu^*)}{2}\sigma^2$$

$$= U(\mu^*) + \frac{U^{(2)}(\mu^*)}{2}\sigma_*^2 + U^{(1)}(\mu^*)(\mu - \mu^*) + \frac{U^{(2)}(\mu^*)}{2}(\sigma^2 - \sigma_*^2),$$

where $\mu = E\{P(\delta)\}$ and $\sigma^2 = \text{Var}\{P(\delta)\}$.

Actually, the reason for Assumptions 5 and 6 was to obtain this inequality, which could be assumed directly instead. It should also be noted that the procedure developed below will still obtain a good feasible solution regardless of whether this inequality holds or not; the inequality is required only to insure that this solution will be optimal.

To reduce this inequality to a more useful form, expand

$$\mu - \mu^* = \sum_{j=1}^{m} \mu_j(\delta_j - \delta_j^*) + \sum_{j=1}^{m} \sum_{\substack{k=1 \\ k \neq j}}^{m} \mu_{jk}(\delta_j \delta_k - \delta_j^* \delta_k^*)$$

$$= \sum_{j=1}^{m} [\mu_j + \sum_{\substack{k=1 \\ k \neq j}}^{m} \mu_{jk}(\delta_k + \delta_k^*)](\delta_j - \delta_j^*),$$

where the second equality holds because $\mu_{jk} = \mu_{kj}$ for all $j$ and $k$ (so that the additional terms cancel).

Now define

$$\Delta_j = \begin{cases} 0, & \text{if } \delta_j - \delta_j^* = 0 \\ 1, & \text{if } |\delta_j - \delta_j^*| = 1, \end{cases}$$

$$\beta_j = \begin{cases} +1, & \text{if } \delta_j^* = 0 \\ -1, & \text{if } \delta_j^* = 1, \end{cases}$$

for $j = 1, ..., m$. Therefore,

$$\mu - \mu^* = \sum_{j=1}^{m} \beta_j [\mu_j + \sum_{\substack{k=1 \\ k \neq j}}^{m} \mu_{jk} \delta_k^* + \sum_{\substack{k \in \{t | \delta_t^* = 0\} \\ k \neq j}} \mu_{jk} \Delta_k + \sum_{\substack{k \in \{t | \delta_t^* = 1\} \\ k \neq j}} \mu_{jk}(1 - \Delta_k)] \Delta_j$$

$$= \sum_{j=1}^{m} \beta_j [\mu_j + 2 \sum_{\substack{k=1 \\ k \neq j}}^{m} \mu_{jk} \delta_k^*] \Delta_j + \sum_{j=1}^{m} \sum_{\substack{k=1 \\ k \neq j}}^{m} \beta_j \beta_k \mu_{jk} \Delta_j \Delta_k.$$

By proceeding in an identical way, it also follows that

$$\sigma^2 - \sigma_*^2 = \sum_{j=1}^{m} \beta_j [\sigma_j^2 + 2 \sum_{\substack{k=1 \\ k \neq j}}^{m} \sigma_{jk} \delta_k^*] \Delta_j + \sum_{j=1}^{m} \sum_{\substack{k=1 \\ k \neq j}}^{m} \beta_j \beta_k \sigma_{jk} \Delta_j \Delta_k.$$

Hence, let

$$a = U(\mu^*) + \frac{U^{(2)}(\mu^*)}{2}\sigma_*^2,$$

$$b_j = U^{(1)}(\mu^*)\beta_j[\mu_j + 2\sum_{\substack{k=1\\k\neq j}}^{m}\mu_{jk}\delta_k^*] + \frac{U^{(2)}(\mu^*)}{2}\beta_j[\sigma_j^2 + 2\sum_{\substack{k=1\\k\neq j}}^{m}\sigma_{jk}\delta_k^*],$$

$$\text{for } j = 1, \ldots, m,$$

$$c_{jk} = U^{(1)}(\mu^*)\beta_j\beta_k\mu_{jk} + \frac{U^{(2)}(\mu^*)}{2}\beta_j\beta_k\sigma_{jk}, \quad \text{for } j, k = 1, \ldots, m(j\neq k),$$

$$g(\varDelta) = a + \sum_{j=1}^{m}b_j\varDelta_j + \sum_{j=1}^{m}\sum_{\substack{k=1\\k\neq j}}^{m}c_{jk}\varDelta_j\varDelta_k,$$

$$f(\varDelta) = E\{U(P(\delta))\},$$

$$F = \{\varDelta|\delta\in S^*\},$$

where

$$\delta_j = \begin{cases} \varDelta_j, & \text{if } \delta_j^* = 0 \\ 1 - \varDelta_j, & \text{if } \delta_j^* = 1 \end{cases}$$

for $j = 1, \ldots, m$. Therefore, the original inequality has now become

$$f(\varDelta) \leqslant g(\varDelta)$$

for $\varDelta \in F$. Notice that $g(\varDelta)$ is of the proper form for the branch-and-bound algorithm presented in Section 6.3. Hence, the original problem may now be solved by using this algorithm to maximize $f(\varDelta)$ over $\varDelta \in F$, and then converting the resulting solution for $\varDelta$ to the equivalent value of $\delta$.

Although this concludes the description of the straightforward version of the exact solution procedure, a few remarks will now be made about possible variations in this procedure.

If Assumptions 5 and/or 6 are not satisfied, so that the above inequality for $E\{U(P(\delta))\}$ may not hold, it is necessary to make some adjustments in order to insure that the solution obtained is optimal. What is required is to obtain an upper bound on the amount by which this inequality can be violated. By adding this upper bound to $g(\Delta)$ for the second sub-problem, the procedure can then be executed just as before, although with some sacrifice in efficiency. Unfortunately, a tight upper bound may not be easy to obtain. If only Assumption 5 is violated, this amounts to finding an upper bound on the remainder term $R$ given in Section 5.2. One such bound is already given there, although a much better one could probably be obtained for any given problem by careful numerical analysis. If Assumption 6 is violated, a good upper bound on the error this introduces should be obtainable by graphical analysis on $U(p)$.

There seem to be a number of possibilities for accelerating the solution procedure under certain circumstances. The efficiency of the branch-and-bound algorithm is affected considerably by the magnitude of $[g(\Delta) - f(\Delta)]$ for $\Delta \in F$, so several of these possibilities involve making adjustments in $g(\Delta)$. Since $g(\Delta) \equiv f(\Delta)$ for the first subproblem, these adjustments would be needed only for the second subproblem. In particular, if Assumption 5 holds, then

$$\max_{\Delta \in F} \{g(\Delta) - f(\Delta)\} = \max_{\delta \in S^*} \left\{ \sum_{k=3}^{\infty} \frac{U^{(k)}(\mu)}{k!} E\{(P(\delta) - \mu)^k\} \right\} \leqslant 0 .$$

Therefore, if an upper bound less than zero can be obtained for this maximum, then this negative number can be safely added to $a$, and there-fore to $g(\Delta)$. This will decrease $B^{(0)}$ in Step 3 of the algorithm, and thereby make it easier for $\max\{B^{(t)}(1), B^{(t)}(0)\}$ to be less than $f^*$ in Step 7.

A related approximate approach would be to use the quantity,

$$\sum_{k=3}^{\infty} \frac{U^{(k)}(\mu^*)}{k!} E\{(P(\delta^*) - \mu^*)^k\} = E\{U(P(\delta^*))\} - U(\mu^*) \frac{U^{(2)}(\mu^*)}{2} \sigma_*^2 ,$$

to add to $g(\Delta)$. This should tend to make $[g(\Delta) - f(\Delta)]$ approximately zero, which would be desirable. Although it is possible that the resulting solution would not be quite optimal, this approximation may be adequate for many practical problems.

A third approach of this kind would be to specify an error tolerance which would then be subtracted from $g(\Delta)$. Thus, the objective would become to find a solution $\delta'$ such that

$$\max_{\delta \in S} \{E\{U(P(\delta))\}\} - E\{U(P(\delta'))\} \leqslant \varepsilon \,,$$

where $\varepsilon$ is the specified allowable error. This would be done by subtracting $\varepsilon$ from $g(\delta)$ and then proceeding just as before.

Still another possibility for accelerating the solution of the second subproblem has been implicitly introduced previously when $S^*$ was used instead of $S$. In other words, the necessary conditions for optimality given in Chapter 2 may be used as a supplementary criterion for rejecting a set of completions. (As a matter of fact, if the necessary assumptions concerning $E\{U(P(\delta))\}$ do not hold, this could be used as the sole criterion except when $f(\varDelta)$ is calculated for an individual solution.) In particular, Corollary 2 to Theorem 3 and maybe Theorem 4 could be applied in a rather straightforward way by carrying along the same upper bound on $E\{P(\delta)\}$ for the current set of completions that is used for the first subproblem. This can be done quite efficiently, especially if most or all of the $\mu_{jk}$ are zero.

There may also be ways to make the branch-and-bound algorithm more efficient for both subproblems. One possibility would be to store each calculated upper bound $B(J_0, J_1, J_N)$ that is above $f^*$, and then begin each iteration by jumping over to the partial solution having the largest such upper bound. This should decrease the number of iterations, although it would also increase both the required computer storage space and the amount of computational effort per iteration.

In concluding this chapter, it should be noted that the solution procedures presented here have not yet been tested in practice. It is anticipated that the approximate procedure will give a good approximation, and that the exact procedure will be reasonably efficient (at least in comparison with other integer programming algorithms). However, it remains to be seen whether this is true, and whether there are variations of these procedures that will do a better job.

CHAPTER 7

# A CHANCE-CONSTRAINED PROGRAMMING APPROACH
# TO A DYNAMIC VERSION OF THE PROBLEM

## 7.1. Formulation

The preceding chapters have considered a static idealization of the
capital budgeting problem whereby $m$ currently available investment
opportunities are considered for approval or rejection on the basis of the
expected utility of their total present value. Thus, at least three dynamic
aspects of the problem have not been taken into account in a completely
satisfactory way. First, since utility is a function of present value only, the
impact of the particular pattern of cash flows over time yielding a given
present value is not fully considered. For example, the possibility of a
large negative present value may be more serious if the entire loss would
occur in one year rather than being spread over a number of years, since
this would provide less opportunity to recoup the losses elsewhere.
Furthermore, if a certain set of investments would have a net cash outflow
in a certain time period that is unacceptably large, then this set would
need to be rejected regardless of whether the subsequent income would
yield a satisfactory present value or not. In principle, this can be partially
taken into account by specifying infeasible solutions, using dependent
random variables, and making the cost of capital a function of $\delta$, but
practical solution procedures would tend to gloss over it. Second, the
impact of other investments, both past and future, are not considered
explicitly. For example, anticipated capital expenditures may indicate a
desirable time table for internally generating funds. This can be partially
incorporated into the analysis by specifying infeasible solutions and

69

adjusting the $i_j$ appropriately, but a more direct approach would be desirable. Furthermore, the existence of other ongoing investments can either increase or decrease the risk of incurring serious overall losses. In principle, this would be taken into account when determining the utility function of present value for the $m$ investments, but it is difficult to do so adequately. Third, rather than only approving or rejecting investments, it would be more realistic to also plan strategies for subsequent actions on these investments. For example, these strategies might involve rules for abandoning unsuccessful investments and switching to new ones, or for increasing the amount invested in a successful project. As suggested in Section 1.6, such possibilities can be allowed for by specifying the alternative strategies in advance and treating them as mutually exclusive investments. However, this is a rather artificial approach that enlarges the size of the problem, and it would be more desirable to let the analysis prescribe the optimal strategy directly.

Despite these shortcomings, the advantages of the simplifying assumptions in this static idealization seem well justified. Considering the difficulty of evaluating risky interrelated investments and the primitive state of the art for doing so, the sacrifice in realism that was made to obtain tractability seems relatively small. Nevertheless, it is evident that alternative approaches which would alleviate these shortcomings also would be of interest. One of these involving chance-constrained programming will be developed in this chapter.

Although the present value criterion will continue to be used, the cash flows occurring in each time period also will be considered explicitly. Appropriate probabilistic constraints will be imposed on these cash flows in order to avoid endangering the short-range financial position. Rather than using a non-linear utility function to eliminate an unacceptably risky set of investments, these constraints will be used to serve this purpose. (This also has the practical advantage of eliminating the onerous task of constructing a utility function.) Therefore, the objective will be to select $\delta \in S$ so as to maximize $E\{P(\delta)\}$, subject to these constraints.

The basic assumptions are those required to reduce this problem to a linear chance-constrained programming problem. In particular, it is assumed that the cash flows, and therefore the present values, emanating from the investments are additive. Thus, if the model of cash flows presented in Chapter 3 is being used, then $h_j(\delta) \equiv 0$ for all $j$ and $\delta$. It is also assumed that, for each $j = 1, \ldots, n$, $i_j(\delta)$ equals a constant $i_j$ for all $\delta \in S$. Thus, $P(\delta) = \sum_{j=1}^{m} P_j \delta_j$ and $E\{P(\delta)\} = \sum_{j=1}^{m} E(P_j)\delta_j$ as in Section 5.1, where $P_j$ is the present value associated with investment $j$. Finally, it is assumed that the constraint, $\delta \in S$, can be expressed in an integer linear programming format, as was discussed in Sections 1.5 and 5.2.

Before proposing the particular mathematical models to be used, a description of the general characteristics of these models is summarized below.

**The general qualitative model**

In general terms, the objective is to choose $\delta = (\delta_1, \ldots, \delta_m)$ so as to

$$\text{maximize} \quad E\{(P(\delta))\} = \sum_{j=1}^{m} E(P_j)\delta_j, \quad \text{subject to}$$

(1) $\text{Prob}\{(NCF)_k \geqslant L_k\} \geqslant \alpha_k$, for $k = 1, \ldots, n$,

(2) $\text{Prob}\{(CNCF)_k \geqslant C_k\} \geqslant \eta_k$, for $k = 2, 3, \ldots, n$,

(3) $\delta \in S$,

where $(NCF)_k$ is the net cash flow in period $k$ and $(CNCF)_k$ is the cumulative net cash flow through period $k$ $(k = 1, \ldots, n)$. Thus, the first set of constraints imposes a lower bound on the net income or, if $L_j$ is negative, an upper bound $(-L_k)$ on the loss in period $k$ $(k = 1, \ldots, n)$, subject to a specified risk level $(1 - \alpha_k)$. The second set of constraints imposes the corresponding bound on the cumulative net cash flow from the present to the end of period $k$ $(k = 2, 3, \ldots, m)$, subject to a specified risk level $(1 - \eta_k)$. Any of these constraints would of course be omitted whenever they are superfluous or irrelevant. "Net cash flow" may be interpreted to include that from other relevant ongoing projects in addition to the $m$ investments under consideration. The bounds would then be established on the basis of the anticipated financial position and need for funds in the respective time periods.

To be more specific, special cases of this model that may be of interest include the three described below. The first two restrict themselves to the class of zero-order decision rules, whereas the third introduces a two-stage formulation that points toward a strategy approach to the problem. Both exact and approximate solution procedures that apply to all three models are given in Section 7.2.

**A basic one-stage model**

Let the random variable $X_{jk}$ be the net cash flow in period $k$ resulting from investment $j$ ($j = 1, ..., m$; $k = 0, 1, ..., n$), and let the random variable $Y_k$ be the net cash flow in period $k$ ($k = 1, ..., n$) from relevant sources other than the $m$ investments. Thus, $Y_k$ represents other cash flows, including those from past and future investments, that are relevant for determining the minimum tolerable net cash flow from the $m$ investments. Alternatively, $Y_k$ can be interpreted as a correction quantity, having a probability distribution based on future business conditions, that should be subtracted from $L_k$.

Thus,

$$E(P_j) = \sum_{k=0}^{n} \frac{E(X_{jk})}{\prod_{t=1}^{k}(1+i_t)}, \quad \text{for} \quad j = 1, ..., m,$$

$$(NCF)_k = Y_k + \sum_{j=1}^{m} X_{jk}\delta_j, \quad \text{for} \quad k = 1, ..., n,$$

$$(CNCF)_k = \sum_{j=1}^{m} X_{j0}\delta_j + \sum_{t=1}^{k}(Y_t + \sum_{j=1}^{m} X_{jt}\delta_j), \quad \text{for} \quad k = 2, 3, ..., n.$$

[This assumes that $Y_k$ includes cash flows from reinvestment; otherwise, $(CNCF)_k$ should be altered by multiplying $\left(Y_k + \sum_{j=1}^{m} X_{jt}\right)$ by $\prod_{l=t+1}^{k}(1+i_l)$.]

**A steady-state model**

Another approach would be to attempt to explicitly include future investments in the analysis. Unfortunately, it often is impossible to predict future investment opportunities with any modicum of accuracy.

Therefore, in the absence of any better information, the most reasonable recourse may be to treat the future as if it will reproduce the present. The model to be formulated here adopts this philosophy that, given no prior information, the best estimate of a future value of a stochastic random variable is its current value. Thus, the model assumes that the investment opportunities available in each successive future period are identical to the current ones in terms of the probability distributions of their cash flows.[1] (Future investments that are identical, in the above sense, to the current investment $j$ will be referred to as "investments of type $j$", where $j = 1, ..., m$.) It is also assumed that the decision $\delta$ selected currently will be repeated in each future period. Thus, this model is designed for finding a "steady-state" solution to the problem. Its rationale is that such a solution should tend to be reasonably consistent with long-range optimization.

Let the random variable $X_{jkl}$ be the net cash flow in period $l$ resulting from an investment of type $j$ that is made in period $k$, and let $P_{jk}$ be the present value of this investment $(j = 1, ..., m; k = 0, 1, ...; l = k, k+1, ..., k+n)$. Let the random variable $Y_k$ be the net cash flow in period $k$ $(k = 1, ..., n)$ from relevant sources other than these current and future investments. Thus, $Y_k$ would be interpreted just as for the basic one-stage model, except that it does not include the cash flows resulting from future investments of types $1, ..., m$. However, it can include cash flows from other special future investments that can be predicted, or cash flows resulting from anticipated expansions in investment opportunities.

Since this model purports to consider the impact of all investments into the indefinite future, the natural objective is to maximize the expected total present value of both current and future investments. Therefore, let $P_j$ be the total present value of all investments (current and future) of type $j$ $(j = 1, ..., m)$. Thus, assuming that $i_t$ equals the same constant $i$ for $t = 1, 2, ...,$

---

[1] However, if any better information about future investment opportunities does happen to be available, the model should be modified accordingly. For example, a "growth curve" effect may be introduced by systematically increasing the scale factor of the probability distributions of cash flow. Other variations can be introduced by means of the $Y_k$ random variables, as will be discussed shortly.

$$P_j = \sum_{k=0}^{\infty} \frac{P_{jk}}{(1+i)^k}, \quad \text{for} \quad j = 1, ..., m.$$

Since $P_{j,0} P_{j,1}, ...$ are identically distributed, it follows (by using the closed form expression for the sum of a geometric series) that

$$E(P_j) = \left(\frac{1+i}{i}\right) E(P_{j0}), \quad \text{for} \quad j = 1, ..., m.$$

(Notice that $E(P_j)$ differs from $E(P_{j0})$ by the same multiplicative constant for all $j$; thus, it would be equivalent to use the expected value of only the current investments, $\sum_{j=1}^{m} E(P_{j0})\delta_j$, for the objective function if desired.)

Therefore, the model now reduces to the desired general form by setting

$$E(P_j) = \frac{1+i}{i} \sum_{k=0}^{n} \frac{E(X_{j0})}{(1+i)^k}, \qquad \text{for} \quad j = 1, ..., m,$$

$$(NCF)_l = Y_l + \sum_{j=1}^{m} \sum_{k=0}^{l} X_{jkl}\delta_j, \qquad \text{for} \quad l = 1, ..., n,$$

$$(CNCF)_l = \sum_{j=1}^{m} X_{j00}\delta_j + \sum_{t=1}^{l} (NCF)_t, \quad \text{for} \quad l = 2, 3, ..., n.$$

The fact that the probabilistic constraints run through to exactly period $n$ is a somewhat arbitrary choice for this particular model, and it may be changed as desired.

## A basic two-stage model

As with the approach used in the preceding chapters, both of the above models are designed for only approving or rejecting investments rather than also planning strategies for subsequent action. Therefore, a model that partially overcomes this shortcoming will now be formulated, based on some recent research on chance-constrained programming done by the author (HILLIER 1967a). In particular, it is assumed that action is taken in two stages. Thus, certain of the decisions would be made immediately (stage 1), and then further action would be taken at a later point in time (stage 2) after learning something about the outcome of the stage 1 decisions.

Let $\delta = (\delta_1, \delta_2, ..., \delta_m)$, as defined and interpreted in Section 1.6, continue to denote the investment decisions that are made at the outset (i.e., at stage 1). Correspondingly, let $m'$ be the number of decisions to be made at stage 2, and let $\Delta = (\Delta_1, \Delta_2, ..., \Delta_{m'})$ denote the second-stage decision vector, where $\Delta_j = 1$ if action $j$ is taken at the second stage, and $\Delta_j = 0$ if it is not ($j = 1, ..., m'$). These second-stage actions would be defined as the situation dictates. For example, if an investment $j$ involves marketing a certain product regionally, then action $k$ might be to market it nationally. (Since this action would be contingent on the investment having been made, $\Delta_k \leqslant \delta_j$ would be introduced as an additional constraint.) As another illustration, action $k$ could be to abandon project (investment) $j$ and switch to project (investment) $l$. (Since this action would be contingent both on investment $j$ being approved and investment $l$ rejected, both $\Delta_k \leqslant \delta_j$ and $\Delta_k \leqslant 1 - \delta_l$ would be introduced as additional constraints.)

For definiteness, assume that the second-stage actions would be taken at the end of the first time period. Let the random variable $X_{jk}$ be the net cash flow in period $k$ resulting from investment $j$ ($j = 1, ..., m$; $k = 0$, $1, ..., n$), given that no action is taken at the second stage. Similarly, let the random variable $W_{jk}$ be the incremental net cash flow in period $k$ resulting from taking action $j$ at the second stage ($j = 1, ..., m'$; $k = 2$, $3, ..., n$). Finally, let the random variable $Y_k$ be the net cash flow in period $k$ ($k = 1, ..., n$) from relevant sources other than the $X_{jk}$ and $W_{jk}$. The interpretation of $Y_k$ is essentially as described for the basic one-stage model.

Thus, the random variables whose value will be known at the second stage are $Y_1, X_{11}, X_{21}, ..., X_{m1}$ (plus $X_{10}, ..., X_{m0}$ if these are random variables rather than constants). Let $V$ be the random vector whose elements are these random variables, and let $n_v$ be the number of elements of $V$. Let $R$ be the range space of $V$, so that $R$ is the set in $n_v$-dimensional Euclidean space consisting of the values that $V$ can take on. Using the rationale described below, $R$ would now be partitioned into $n_r$ disjoint subsets, $R_1, R_2, ..., R_{n_r}$, whose union is $R$. Let

$$p_l = \text{Prob}\{V \in R_l\}, \quad \text{for} \quad l = 1, ..., n_r.$$

For each $l = 1, ..., n_r$, let $Y_1^{(l)}, ..., Y_n^{(l)}, X_{10}^{(l)}, ..., X_{mn}^{(l)}, W_{12}^{(l)}, ..., W_{m'n}^{(l)}$ be the set of random variables whose joint probability distribution coincides with the conditional joint distribution of $Y_1, ..., Y_n, X_{10}, ..., X_{mn}, W_{12}, ..., W_{m'n}$, given that $V \in R_l$.

Given the above development, the choice of $\Delta$ can now be made conditional upon the identity of the subset of $R$ which contains the value taken on by $V$. Thus, for each $l = 1, ..., n_r$, let $\Delta^{(l)} = (\Delta_1^{(l)}, ..., \Delta_{m'}^{(l)})$ denote the value of $\Delta$ that will be chosen if $V \in R_l$. Let $E\{P(\delta, \Delta^{(1)}, ..., \Delta^{(n_r)})\}$ be the expected total present value resulting from specifying $\delta, \Delta^{(1)}, ..., \Delta^{(n_r)}$. The resulting formulation of the problem is to determine $\delta, \Delta^{(1)}, ..., \Delta^{(n_r)}$ so as to

$$\max E\{P(\delta, \Delta^{(1)}, ..., \Delta^{(n_r)})\} = \sum_{j=1}^{m} E(P_j)\delta_j + \sum_{l=1}^{n_r} p_l \sum_{j=1}^{m'} E(P_j^{(l)})\Delta_j^{(l)},$$

subject to

(1a) $\text{Prob}\{NCF)_1 \geq L_1\} \geq \alpha_1$,

(1b) $\text{Prob}\{(NCF)_k^{(l)} \geq L_k\} \geq \alpha_k$, for $k = 2, 3, ..., n$; $l = 1, ..., n_r$,

(2) $\text{Prob}\{(CNCF)_k^{(l)} \geq C_k\} \geq \eta_k$, for $k = 2, 3, ..., n$; $l = 1, ..., n_r$,

(3) $(\delta, \Delta^{(l)}) \in S'$, for $l = 1, ..., n_r$,

where

$$E(P_j) = \sum_{k=0}^{n} \frac{E(X_{jk})}{\prod\limits_{t=1}^{k}(1+i_t)}, \quad \text{for } j = 1, ..., m,$$

$$E(P_j^{(l)}) = \sum_{k=2}^{n} \frac{E(W_{jk}^{(l)})}{\prod\limits_{t=1}^{k}(1+i_t)}, \quad \text{for } j = 1, ..., m'; \ l = 1, ..., n_r,$$

$$(NCF)_1 = Y_1 + \sum_{j=1}^{m} X_{jk}\delta_j,$$

$$(NCF)_k^{(l)} = Y_k^{(l)} + \sum_{j=1}^{m} X_{jk}^{(l)}\delta_j + \sum_{j=1}^{m'} W_{jk}^{(l)}\Delta_j^{(l)},$$

$$\text{for } k = 2, 3, ..., n; \ l = 1, ..., n_r,$$

$$(CNCF)_k^{(l)} = \sum_{t=1}^{k} Y_t^{(l)} + \sum_{t=0}^{k}\sum_{j=1}^{m} X_{jk}^{(l)}\delta_j + \sum_{t=2}^{k}\sum_{j=1}^{m'} W_{jt}^{(l)}\Delta_j^{(l)},$$

$$\text{for } k = 2, 3, ..., n; \ l = 1, ..., n_r,$$

and where $S'$ is the set of feasible solutions for $(\delta, \Delta)$.

Despite its complicated appearance, this model is also merely a special case (with some change in notation) of the general qualitative model presented earlier. Therefore, it too can be solved by the solution procedures given in the next section.

As indicated elsewhere by the author (HILLIER 1967a), the main consideration when partitioning $R$ is that the points within a subset should be as similar as possible in their impact upon what the second-stage decisions should be, whereas points in different subsets should be as different as possible in this regard. To illustrate, suppose that the relevant new information for deciding on the second-stage actions is how well the overall set of investments approved at the first stage is turning out. One might then construct, for example, five categories–much worse than expected, somewhat worse than expected, about as expected, somewhat better than expected, and much better than expected. Ranges of values of $V$ would be matched up with these categories and thereby assigned to the five subsets, $R_1, ..., R_5$. Similarly, if the outcomes of certain individual investments, or groups of interrelated investments, are also particularly desirable, it might be desirable to use combinations of such categories to obtain the subsets. The main restriction is that the total number of subsets must be small enough to keep the problem manageable in terms of analysis and computational effort, so the partitioning may need to be more coarse than desired. However, even a coarse partitioning may yield considerably more guidance on which current and future investment decisions are most compatible with long-range optimization than can the models considered previously.

## 7.2. Exact and approximate solution procedures

All of the models formulated in Section 7.1 are ordinary chance-constrained programming problems with 0–1 decision variables. Solution procedures for this type of problem were recently developed elsewhere by the author (HILLIER 1967a). However, for the convenience of the reader, these procedures will be summarized here, although without the proofs and discussion to be found in that paper.

Each probabilistic constraint is of the form,

$$\text{Prob}\left\{ \sum_{j=1}^{m} a_j \delta_j \leqslant b \right\} \geqslant \beta \,,$$

where $a_1, \ldots, a_m, b$ all may be random variables. For example, the $k$th constraint of type 1 for the basic one-stage model is

$$\text{Prob}\left\{ Y_k + \sum_{j=1}^{m} X_{jk} \delta_k \geqslant L \right\} \geqslant \alpha_k \,,$$

which is equivalent to

$$\text{Prob}\left\{ \sum_{j=1}^{m} (-X_{jk}) \delta_j \leqslant Y_k - L_k \right\} \geqslant \alpha_k \,,$$

which is of this form. Therefore, each probabilistic constraint should be modified as described below for a typical constraint.

Define

$$\sigma^2 = \sum_{j=1}^{m} \text{Var}(a_j) + \text{Var}(b) \,,$$

$$\sigma_j^2 = \text{Var}(a_j), \qquad \text{for} \quad j = 1, \ldots, m \,,$$

$$\sigma_{jk} = \text{Cov}(a_j, a_k), \quad \text{for} \quad j, k = 1, \ldots, m \; (j \neq k) \,.$$

The first step is to replace the constraint by its deterministic equivalent,

$$\sum_{j=1}^{m} E(a_j) \delta_j + K_\beta \sqrt{\text{Var}\left\{ \sum_{j=1}^{m} a_j \delta_j - b \right\}} \leqslant E(b) \,,$$

where $K_\beta$ is the $\beta$-fractile[1] of the general probability distribution[2] of $\left( \sum_{j=1}^{m} a_j \delta_j - b \right)$ when this distribution has mean zero and variance one.

---

[1] The $\beta$-fractile of a distribution is the number such that the fraction of the distribution lying below it is $\beta$. It is assumed that $\beta$ is sufficiently large (approximately above $\frac{1}{2}$) so that $K_\beta \geqslant 0$.

[2] It is assumed that this general distribution is the same, e.g., normal, for all $\delta$, and that its fractiles depend only on the mean and variance.

The next step depends upon whether $a_1, ..., a_m, b$ are statistically independent or not, so these two cases will be considered separately.

Assume initially that $a_1, ..., a_m, b$ are mutually independent. It can
then be shown that, since the $\delta_j$ are restricted to values of zero or one,

$$\sqrt{\text{Var}\left\{\sum_{j=1}^{m} a_j\delta_j - b\right\}} \leqslant f(\delta),$$

where

$$f(\delta) = \sigma - \sum_{j=1}^{m}\left[\sigma - \sqrt{\sigma^2 - \sigma_j^2}\right](1 - \delta_j).$$

If $\delta$ is further restricted to values such that $\sum_{j=1}^{m}\delta_j \leqslant m_1 < m - 1$, it also follows that

$$\sqrt{\text{Var}\left\{\sum_{j=1}^{m} a_j\delta_j - b\right\}} \leqslant f(\delta) - c,$$

where

$$c = \sigma - \sum_{j\in J}\left[\sigma - \sqrt{\sigma^2 - \sigma_j^2}\right] - \sqrt{\sigma^2 - \sum_{j\in J}\sigma_j^2},$$

where the set $J$ contains the values of $j$ corresponding to the $(m - m_1)$
smallest values of $\sigma_j^2$ $(j = 1, ..., m)$. Therefore, the deterministic equivalent
of the constraint can be replaced by a uniformly tighter linear constraint

merely by replacing $\sqrt{\text{Var}\left\{\sum_{j=1}^{m} a_j\delta_j - b\right\}}$ by its linear upper bound given

above. To obtain a uniformly looser linear constraint instead, let $v$ be
the number such that

$$\sqrt{\text{Var}(b)} + \sum_{j=1}^{m}\left[\sqrt{v} - \sqrt{v - \sigma_j^2}\right] = \sigma,$$

as can be found by numerical methods. (Any tight upper bound on $v$ also
could be used instead.) It then follows that

$$g(\delta, v) \leqslant \sqrt{\text{Var}\left\{\sum_{j=1}^{m} a_j\delta_j - b\right\}},$$

where

$$g(\delta, v) = \sqrt{\mathrm{Var}(b)} + \sum_{j=1}^{m} \left[ \sqrt{v} - \sqrt{v - \sigma_j^2} \right] \delta_j.$$

Thus, replacing $\sqrt{\mathrm{Var}\left\{ \sum_{j=1}^{m} a_j \delta_j - b \right\}}$ by $g(\delta, v)$ provides a uniformly looser constraint.

The way in which the uniformly tighter and uniformly looser linear constraints are used in the solution procedures will be described shortly.

Now consider the case where $a_1, \ldots, a_m, b$ are not mutually independent. Define

$$c_j = K_\beta^2 \sigma_j^2 - [E(a_j)]^2 + 2E(b)E(a_j) - K_\beta^2 \, \mathrm{Cov}(a_j, b), \text{ for } j = 1, \ldots, m,$$

$$d_{jk} = K_\beta^2 \, \mathrm{Cov}(a_j, a_k) - E(a_j)E(a_k), \text{ for } j, k = 1, \ldots, m \, (j \neq k),$$

$$r = [E(b)]^2 - K_\beta^2 \, \mathrm{Var}(b).$$

Then the constraint,

$$\sum_{j=1}^{m} E(a_j) \delta_j + K_\beta \sqrt{\mathrm{Var} \left\{ \sum_{j=1}^{m} a_j \delta_j - b \right\}} \leqslant E(b),$$

is equivalent to, and should be replaced by, the pair of constraints,

$$\sum_{j=1}^{m} c_j \delta_j + \sum_{j=1}^{m} \sum_{\substack{k=1 \\ k \neq j}}^{m} d_{jk} \delta_j \delta_k \leqslant r,$$

$$\sum_{j=1}^{m} E(a_j) \delta_j \leqslant E(b).$$

Therefore, in order to obtain a set of uniformly tighter or uniformly looser linear constraints, it is only necessary to replace $\sum_{j=1}^{m} \sum_{\substack{k=1 \\ k \neq j}}^{m} d_{jk} \delta_j \delta_k$ by a linear upper bound and linear lower bound, respectively. Such bounds are given below.

For each $j = 1, \ldots, m$, let $(p_j^{(1)}, \ldots, p_j^{(m-1)})$ be a permutation of $\{1, \ldots, j-1, j+1, \ldots, m\}$ such that $d_{j, p_j^{(1)}} \geqslant d_{j, p_j^{(2)}} \geqslant \ldots \geqslant d_{j, p_j^{(m-1)}}$. For any given integers, $m_0$ and $m_1$, such that $0 \leqslant m_0 \leqslant m_1 \leqslant m$, define

$$e_j = \sum_{\substack{k=1 \\ k \neq j}}^{m} d_{jk} + \sum_{k=m-m_0+1}^{m-1} \max\{d_{j,p^{(k)}}, 0\} + \sum_{k=m-m_1}^{m-1} \min\{d_{j,p^{(k)}_j}, 0\},$$

$$u_j = e_j - \sum_{\substack{k=1 \\ k \neq j}}^{m} (d_{jk} + \min\{d_{jk}, 0\}),$$

$$x_j = \sum_{k=1}^{m_0-1} d_{j,p^{(k)}_j} + \sum_{k=m_0}^{m_1} \max\{d_{j,p^{(k)}_j}, 0\},$$

$$q_j = \sum_{k=1}^{m_0-1} d_{j,p^{(m-k)}_j} + \sum_{k=m_0}^{m_1-1} \min\{d_{j,p^{(m-k)}_j}, 0\},$$

for $j = 1, \ldots, m$, and let $s$ be the sum of the $(m-m_1)$ smallest elements of $(u_1, \ldots, u_m)$. It can be shown that

$$\sum_{j=1}^{m} \sum_{\substack{k=1 \\ k \neq j}}^{m} d_{jk} \delta_j \delta_k \leq h_1(\delta),$$

where

$$h_1(\delta) = \sum_{j=1}^{m} \sum_{\substack{k=1 \\ k \neq j}}^{m} d_{jk} - \sum_{j=1}^{m} \left[ \sum_{\substack{k=1 \\ k \neq j}}^{m} (d_{jk} + \min\{d_{jk}, 0\}) \right] (1 - \delta_j).$$

Furthermore, if $\delta \in S$ implies that $m_0 \leq \sum_{j=1}^{m} \delta_j \leq m_1$, then

$$\sum_{j=1}^{m} \sum_{\substack{k=1 \\ k \neq j}}^{m} d_{jk} \delta_j \delta_k \leq \sum_{j=1}^{m} \sum_{\substack{k=1 \\ k \neq j}}^{m} d_{jk} - \sum_{j=1}^{m} e_j(1 - \delta_j),$$

$$\sum_{j=1}^{m} \sum_{\substack{k=1 \\ k \neq j}}^{m} d_{jk} \delta_j \delta_k \leq h_1(\delta) - s,$$

$$\sum_{j=1}^{m} \sum_{\substack{k=1 \\ k \neq j}}^{m} d_{jk} \delta_j \delta_k \leq \sum_{j=1}^{m} \gamma_j \delta_j,$$

and

$$\sum_{j=1}^{m} q_j \delta_j \leq \sum_{j=1}^{m} \sum_{\substack{k=1 \\ k \neq j}}^{m} d_{jk} \delta_j \delta_k.$$

Given the above results [which are evaluated and compared elsewhere (HILLIER 1967a)], both approximately and exactly optimal solutions can now be obtained. Consider first how to find a good suboptimal solution.

Probably the most attractive approach is to apply linear programming. To begin, replace the deterministic equivalent form of the probabilistic constraints by uniformly tighter linear constraints, as discussed above, and replace the restriction that $\delta_j = 0$ or 1 by $0 \leqslant \delta_j \leqslant 1$ for $j = 1, ..., m$. Then solve the resulting linear programming problem by the simplex method, and apply sensitivity analysis and duality theory to analyze the problem as desired. (Parametric programming techniques may also be applied at this point to obtain a better solution to the original problem by loosening the constraints. See HILLIER 1967a, for a detailed discussion.) The last step is to modify the final linear programming solution by rounding the fractional variables up or down in such a way as to obtain a feasible solution to the original problem with a relatively large value of the objective function. Fortunately, WEINGARTNER (1963, pp. 35 ff.) has shown that the number of fractional variables cannot exceed the number of functional constraints, so this may not be a difficult task. (If this is too difficult, an alternative approach is to retain the integer restriction and apply an integer linear programming algorithm, preferably an efficient suboptimal one such as those developed by the author (HILLIER 1966a)). Furthermore, since the final solution needs to be feasible only for the original problem, and not for the approximating linear programming problem, it may even be possible to increase the value of the objective function.

If it is necessary to find an optimal solution, one may proceed as follows. First, find a good suboptimal solution by the method described above. Next, replace the deterministic equivalent form of the probabilistic constraints by uniformly looser constraints, as described earlier. This yields an ordinary integer linear programming problem. The final step is to apply a slightly modified version of a bound-and-scan algorithm developed by the author (HILLIER 1966b) for this problem, where the suboptimal solution found above would be used to start the algorithm. The one modification is that each new "better feasible solution" found by the algorithm should be discarded if it is not feasible for the original chance-constrained programming problem. The final solution accepted by the algorithm would then be the optimal solution to the original problem.

# CHAPTER 8

# SUMMARY AND CONCLUSIONS

This book has studied the problem of evaluating a proposed set of risky interrelated investments, using present value and expected utility of present value as criteria. The investigation began by deriving properties that characterize an optimal combination of investments, and then a model was developed for describing the interrelated cash flows generated by a set of investments. This model would be used for determining the mean, variance, and possibly the functional form of the probability distribution of present value. The question of when this distribution would be normal or approximately normal was explored in detail. Finally, several models were formulated for finding the expected utility of approving any particular combination of investments. Given these results, an approximate linear programming approach and an exact branch-and-bound algorithm were then developed for selecting the investments to be made.

The problem also was studied in a broader dynamic context. This led to the formulation of several chance-constrained programming models for maximizing expected present value subject to probabilistic constraints on the allowable risk. Both approximate and exact solution procedures were described.

The relative desirability of these two approaches depends upon the prevailing circumstances. The main relative advantages of the expected utility approach is that it provides a more fundamental and precise evaluation of the overall merit of the investments, and that it can readily take into account competitive or complementary interactions between pairs of investments. On the other hand, the chance-constrained programming approach may be easier to implement, and it gives fuller consideration to certain dynamic aspects of the problem (as discussed at the beginning of Chapter 7). Thus, a choice between the two would be dictated by the relative importance of these considerations.

However, in many circumstances, it might well be that the best course of action would be to apply both approaches. In theory, an "optimal" solution may be obtained after one application of one approach. However, this solution would of course be optimal only for the idealized model, and much additional analysis may be required before a final decision is made on which investments to approve. In particular, two aspects of the problem especially need further consideration. First, since much of the input data may be based only on rough subjective estimates, an extensive sensitivity analysis may be desirable. This process would involve identifying the input parameters that are especially critical in determining the model solution, checking the reasonableness of the solutions obtained by varying these parameters, and then attempting to improve the critical estimates and converge to a solution that better reflects the realities of the problem. Second, relevant considerations that could not be incorporated into the model should be analyzed carefully and the solution modified accordingly. This is where the "other" approach might play a useful role. Each approach incorporates certain considerations not contained in the other. Therefore, comparing the solutions yielded by the two approaches, and trying to resolve their differences, may lead to a better solution than by carrying through the entire analysis with only one approach. This of course requires considerably more analytical time and effort, but it may be justified in some cases.

A third approach that has become somewhat popular since it was proposed in 1964 by HERTZ is to use simulation to estimate the probability distribution of present value (or other measures). Simulation has the advantages of being versatile and easy to understand, so it has been a natural first-generation approach to risk analysis. Unfortunately, it has a number of serious disadvantages which make it poorly suited for the analysis of risky interrelated investments. One of the lesser of these is that simulation is inherently an imprecise technique, even with respect to the model used, since it provides only statistical estimates rather than exact results. In other applications, these estimates commonly are of the mean of a distribution, in which case the ones yielded by the usual computer run sizes tend to have a low but tolerable precision. However, estimates of probability distributions are considerably more crude, especially when a tail of the distribution is critical, as is the case here. Estimates of differences between alternatives also are at least as imprecise. Furthermore, simulation is a cumbersome way to study a problem, since it requires developing the model and input data, and then doing the computer programming and executing the computer runs. However, perhaps the most critical disadvantage is that simulation yields only numerical data about the predicted performance of investments, so that it yields no additional insight into cause-and-effect relationships. Therefore, every slightly new case must be completely rerun. This, in addition to the imprecision, tends to make it impossible to conduct a satisfactory sensitivity analysis. An even more serious implication is that a new simulation run is required for each combination of interrelated investments under consideration. Since even one run of acceptable length is expensive, and there may be thousands or even millions of feasible combinations, this too would tend to be prohibitively expensive. Finally, even if one were able to obtain a crude estimate of the probability distribution of present value for each of these feasible combinations, the simulation approach provides no guidance on how to use all of these masses of data in order to select the investments to be approved. For all of these reasons, simulation has been discarded in this paper in favor of the superior approaches to evaluating risky interrelated investments that are described herein.

There seem to be a number of interesting areas for future research on this problem. Perhaps the most crucial one is to develop improved procedures for handling dynamic aspects of the problem, such as those discussed at the beginning of Chapter 7. In particular, a strategy approach to making sequential investment decisions would be very useful. Another worthwhile generalization would be to permit fractional investments. Thus, rather than only approving or rejecting investments of predetermined size, the magnitude of the immediate commitment to each project also would be incorporated into the decision variable. As indicated elsewhere (HILLIER 1967a), the chance-constrained programming approach extends readily to this case, and it appears that some of the other results given here may also generalize. A third area for research would be to develop comparable results for criteria other than present value and expected utility of present value, especially criteria that are particularly designed for considering risk. Another promising area would be to further develop the chance-constrained programming approach introduced in Chapter 7. For example, it would be interesting to attempt to parallel the entire development of WEINGARTNER (1963), including the use of the dual problem for interpretive purposes and his treatment of capital budgeting under imperfect capital markets. When fractional investments are permitted, linear decision rules (e.g., see CHARNES and COOPER 1959a, 1959b, 1962b, 1963, and HILLIER 1967a) also could be used to improve the sequential decision process. Finally, it would be worthwhile to do computational experimentation on the solution procedures presented in Chapters 6 and 7 in order to evaluate, compare, and improve them.

It is hoped that this book will provide a theoretical foundation for the practical evaluation of risky interrelated investments, and that it will stimulate more research in this vital area.

# SUGGESTIONS ON IMPLEMENTATION

## A.1. A useful model for estimating cash flows

In order to determine the probability distribution of present value, it is necessary to know the probability distribution (or at least the mean and variance) of each of the individual cash flows ($Y_{j_{kl}}$ and $\sigma_{j_{kl}} Z_{jl}$ for the model of Chapter 3). In a practical setting, this may require that an analyst describe a subjective probability distribution for each of these cash flows. It may be unrealistic to expect him to provide a complete description. Therefore, the model described below will specify a general type of probability distribution which seems reasonable for cash flows. The analyst will then be required to make three readily comprehendable types of estimates which will completely determine the specific probability distribution for each cash flow. This procedure has the additional advantage that it is patterned after the PERT technique (MALCOLM *et al.* 1959). This technique has achieved considerable success in evaluating research and development program schedules, so that its procedures are well known and widely accepted in industry (although many question its theoretical basis).

The suggested estimating procedure is to make an "optimistic" estimate, a "pessimistic" estimate, and a "most likely" estimate for each cash flow. The nature of these estimates should be just what their names imply. The optimistic estimate of cash flow assumes that "everything will go as well as reasonably possible". The pessimistic estimate of cash flow assumes that "everything will go as poorly as reasonably possible". The third estimate is of the amount of net cash flow that is most likely to occur.

It is assumed that these estimates correspond to the lower bound, upper bound, and mode, respectively, of the probability distribution. It is further assumed that an adequate model for the form of this distribution is the Beta distribution such that the standard deviation is $\frac{1}{6}$ of the spread between the lower bound and upper bound. The Beta distribution somewhat resembles the normal distribution, but there are two differences to be noted. The Beta distribution is bounded in the tails instead of going off to $\pm\infty$ as does the normal distribution. Furthermore, the Beta distribution need not be symmetrical. It will be skewed appropriately if the mode is not midway between the bounds. Thus, the most likely estimate is free to take any position between the optimistic and pessimistic estimates, depending entirely on the analyst's judgment. However, if he does select the most likely value midway between the extreme values, the resulting distribution is nearly normal with the extreme estimates lying three standard deviations away from the mean.

The concepts of an "optimistic estimate", a "pessimistic estimate", and a "most likely estimate" should be relatively simple to understand and use. It would probably only confuse the analyst if these intuitively meaningful ideas were replaced, or even supplemented, by technically precise definitions. However, insomuch as the terms, "optimistic" and "pessimistic", may be slightly ambiguous, some guidelines as to their interpretation will be suggested. The optimistic/pessimistic estimate should be interpreted as the estimate of the maximum/minimum value that could occur. It should not be interpreted as an optimistic/pessimistic estimate of the most likely value. However, once this maximum/minimum concept has been made clear, a slight disclaimer should be inserted. While the model of an underlying Beta distribution has been assumed, it should be recognized that this is only an assumption. The actual underlying distribution may be essentially unbounded, which would lead to an extremely large spread between estimates of the maximum and minimum values. Actually, the location of the bounds of the true underlying distribution is not particularly important. Rather, the extremely vital requirement is that the spread between the pessimistic and optimistic estimates should represent about six standard deviations for the actual distribution. Therefore, to help insure that this goal will still be achieved should the actual distribution be, say, normal, the optimistic and pessimistic estimates should ignore extremely unlikely "windfalls" or catastrophic events. Hence, the optimistic/pessimistic estimate should represent a reasonable maximum/minimum value for which there may still be "one chance in several hundred" of being exceeded in the positive/negative direction.

Under the assumption that each cash flow has a Beta distribution with a spread of six standard deviations between the bounds, the mean and variance are explicit functions of the bounds and mode. These functions are given by MALCOLM *et al.* (1959). To reproduce these results in the present context with a minimum of repetition, let $W$ denote any individual cash flow. Given estimates of the bounds and mode of $W$, i.e., given an "optimistic" estimate, $\text{Est}_o\{W\}$, a "pessimistic" estimate, $\text{Est}_p\{W\}$, and a "most likely" estimate, $\text{Est}_m\{W\}$, the desired estimates of the mean and variance of $W$ are

$$\text{Est}\{E(W)\} \doteq \tfrac{1}{3}[2\,\text{Est}_m\{W\} + \tfrac{1}{2}(\text{Est}_p\{W\} + \text{Est}_o\{W\})]$$

and

$$\text{Est}\{\text{Var}(W)\} = [\tfrac{1}{6}(\text{Est}_o\{W\} - \text{Est}_p\{W\})]^2 .$$

## A.2. A useful model for correlation patterns

While it would occasionally be reasonable to consider all cash flows to be mutually independent (in a statistical sense), there often exist underlying factors which influence some of the cash flows in a comparable manner. In other words, cash flows (such as those described in Chapter 3) often are statistically correlated. Such correlation must be specified in order to correctly calculate the variance of present value. Although this could be done in principle by directly estimating the correlation coefficient for each pair of random variables, the number of pairs tends to be much too large for this approach to be practical. Therefore, the objective here will be to develop a model for the pattern of correlations between cash flows which is both reasonable and sufficiently simple to be compatible with the limitations of the estimating and computing processes. This model will permit inferring the values for all of the correlation coefficients on the basis of estimated values for only a small proportion of them. These few required estimates can then be made by a method described in Section A.4.

One type of correlation pattern to be specified is the correlation between cash flows of the same type in different time periods. If the model of Chapter 3 were being used, this would refer to the correlation between random variables in the sequence, $Y_{1kl}, Y_{2kl}, ..., Y_{nkl}$, or $Z_{1l}, Z_{2l}, ..., Z_{nl}$. The same general assumptions will be made about all such sequences, so consider only the $\{Y_{jkl}\}$ sequence explicitly for purposes of discussion. It would usually be reasonable to expect that $Y_{jkl}$ would be more highly correlated with its predecessor, $Y_{(j-1)kl}$, than with even earlier random variables in the sequence. It is likely that the specific circumstances that would tend to push the amount of net cash flow above or below expectations in one time period would tend to have a greater influence on subsequent cash flow that occurs in the near future than that which occurs in the distant future. To go one step further, it still seems likely that the specific circumstances that affect cash flow in the time period $(j-1)$ would influence cash flow in time period $t$, where $t > j$, only inasmuch as this influence was carried over from time period $j$. To be more precise, it seems likely that the random variables in the sequence would be Markov-dependent. Therefore, the first assumption is that this is indeed the case, so that the conditional probability distribution of $Y_{jkl}$, given $Y_{1kl}, Y_{2kl}, ...,$ $Y_{(j-1)kl}$, is the same as the conditional distribution of $Y_{jkl}$, given only $Y_{(j-1)kl}$. Thus, $Y_{jkl}$ depends on $Y_{1kl}, Y_{2kl}, ..., Y_{(j-2)kl}$ only through $Y_{(j-1)kl}$; $Y_{jkl}$, given $Y_{(j-1)kl}$, is independent of $Y_{1kl}, ..., Y_{(j-2)kl}$. In statistical terminology, this says that the partial correlation coefficient between $Y_{jkl}$ and $Y_{tkl}$ $(t = 1, 2, ..., j-2)$ with respect to $Y_{(j-1)kl}$ is zero; i.e., after removing variation due to $Y_{(j-1)kl}$, $Y_{jkl}$ is independent of $Y_{tkl}$.

The assumption will also be made that the total correlation coefficient between $Y_{(j-1)kl}$ and $Y_{jkl}$ equals the same constant over all $j$ $(j = 2, 3, ..., n)$.

Given the above assumptions, it is now possible to determine the total correlation coefficient between $Y_{jst}$ and $Y_{kst}$ for all $j$ and $k$ $(j,k = 1, 2, ..., n)$ as soon as an estimate of its value for one $j$ and $k = j-1$ is provided. For given values of $s$ and $t$, let $\rho_{jk}$ denote the total correlation coefficient of $Y_{jst}$ and $Y_{kst}$, let $\rho = \rho_{j(j-1)}$, and let $\rho_{jk \cdot l}$ denote the partial correlation coefficient of $Y_{jst}$ and $Y_{kst}$ with respect to $Y_{lst}$. ANDERSON (1958, p. 34) exhibits the relationship between partial and total correlation coefficients as

$$\rho_{jk \cdot l} = \frac{\rho_{jk} - \rho_{jl} \rho_{kl}}{\sqrt{1 - \rho_{jl}^2} \sqrt{1 - \rho_{kl}^2}}.$$

It has been assumed that $\rho_{jk\cdot(k-1)}=0$ for $j<k-1$. Therefore, when $l=k-1$ and $j<k-1$, then

$$\rho_{jk}=\rho_{j(k-1)}\rho_{k(k-1)}$$

$$=\rho_{j(k-1)}\rho \ .$$

Thus, $\rho_{(k-2)k}=\rho^2$, another substitution yields $\rho_{(k-3)k}=\rho^3$, etc. Therefore, the desired result is

$$\rho_{jk}=\rho^{|k-j|} \ .$$

The second type of correlation pattern to be specified is the correlation between cash flows of different types. For the model of Chapter 3, this would mean between $Y_{jkl}$ and $Y_{rst}$ or between $Z_{jk}$ and $Z_{tl}$ (since the $Z_{tl}$ random variables are functions of exogenous variables, they are already known to be independent of the $Y_{jkl}$ random variables). A considerable simplification will again be achieved by making a natural assumption about most of these relationships. Using $\{Y_{jkl}\}$ again for illustrative purposes, this assumption is that the partial correlation coefficient between $Y_{jlr}$ and $Y_{kst}$ $(k<j,\ l\neq s$ or $r\neq t)$ with respect to $Y_{jst}$ is zero. It says that a cash flow in a given time period, given a different type of cash flow in the same time period, is independent of the latter type of cash flow in an earlier time period. It would describe the usual situation where the circumstances that tend to push several types of cash flow up or down would affect these cash flows nearly simultaneously rather than in different time periods.

The assumption will also be made that the total correlation coefficient between $Y_{jlr}$ and $Y_{jst}$ is a constant over all values of $j$ $(j=1, 2, ..., n;$ $l\neq s$ or $r\neq t)$.

To illustrate how to find the total correlation coefficient between $Y_{jlr}$ and $Y_{kst}$, let $\rho_{jk}^*$ denote this parameter for given values of $l, r, s,$ and $t$, and let $\rho^*=\rho_{jj}^*$. Using the relationship between partial correlation coefficients and total correlation coefficients given in a preceding paragraph,

$$\rho_{jk}^*=\rho_{jk}\rho^*$$

$$=\rho^{|k-j|}\rho^* \ ,$$

where $\rho_{jk}$ and $\rho$ are as defined earlier. Thus, $\rho_{jk}^*$ can be calculated for all $j$ and $k$ after estimating only $\rho^*$ and $\rho$.

### A.3. Structuring the problem

Given *m* proposed investments, the analyst must identify the distinct sources of cash flow from each one as well as the relevant exogenous variables. Little can be said in general about this procedure except to emphasize that good judgment and moderation should be exercised. It would usually be possible to divide and further subdivide the cash flows resulting from an investment into an extremely long list of slightly different sources. An extremely long list of exogenous variables of all degrees of importance and relevance could also be generated. However, it should be kept in mind that this decomposition of total cash flows is a means to an end and not an end in itself. Its purposes are to decompose the large, complex task of estimating total cash flows into smaller, more manageable tasks, and to thereby increase the accuracy and efficiency of the estimating process. There will inevitably be a point where the diminishing advantages of further decomposition no longer justify the resulting increase in the amount of estimating and computing time required. The analyst should seek the point which provides the best combination of convenience and accuracy.

Other basic questions are the appropriate length of a time period and the number of time periods (*n*) to be considered. The usual convention is to use a year as the length of a time period. While there is nothing sacred about this convention, it is commonly a reasonable one. However, should the interest rate be low and the cash flows quite stable over time, a longer time period would not sacrifice much accuracy and therefore might be justified by the resulting decrease in estimating and computing time. On the other hand, if the interest rate is high and the cash flows vary rapidly over time, a significant increase in accuracy might be obtained by using a shorter time period. This is a judgment decision which should seek an economic balance between the accuracy of the solution and the effort required to obtain it. The same considerations are involved in the selection of *n*. In principle, one should select the value of *n* such that the *n*th time period is the last time period in which there is a positive probability of a non-zero cash flow resulting from any of the investments. This is certainly appropriate if there is a definite scheduled time in the relatively near future when all cash flows are terminated. However, many investments are open-ended in the sense that they may generate cash flows almost indefinitely under the proper circumstances. As a practical matter, it is undesirable from the standpoint of the estimating and computing effort involved to make $n$ extremely large in order to include possible small cash flows in the distant future. Furthermore, considering the time value of money, distant cash flows have to be discounted to such a small fraction of their value that they contribute relatively little to present value. Therefore, it becomes reasonable to arbitrarily truncate the study period at a point where later cash flows are so small and so far in the future that they would not contribute significantly to present value. This truncation may be somewhat compensated for by including subsequent cash flow, properly discounted, with the estimated cash flow in the $n$th time period.

## A.4. Estimation of correlation coefficients

Assume that $W_1$ and $W_2$ are two random variables with variances, $\sigma_1^2$ and $\sigma_2^2$, respectively, and with a correlation coefficient of $\rho$. For purposes of initial discussion, assume that the joint probability distribution of $W_1$ and $W_2$ is a bivariate normal distribution.

It is well known (e.g., see MOOD 1950, p. 169) that

$$E(W_2 | W_1 = w) = E(W_2) + \rho(\sigma_2/\sigma_1)(w - E(W_1)).$$

Rewriting this expression,

$$\frac{E(W_2 | W_1 = w) - E(W_2)}{\sigma_2} = \rho \frac{w - E(W_1)}{\sigma_1}.$$

In other words, after normalizing $W_1$ and $W_2$, the expected value of $W_2$, given the value of $W_1$, is just $\rho$ times the value of $W_1$. This provides a reasonably simple basis for developing a subjective estimate of $\rho$. Given that the value of $W_1$ lies $k$ standard deviations above its mean, the expected value of $W_2$ will lie $\rho k$ standard deviations above its unconditional mean. By trying various positive and negative values of $k$ and estimating the corresponding conditional expected value of $W_2$, a judgment can be made on the appropriate subjective estimate of $\rho$.

Unfortunately, the problem of concern here is the estimation of the correlation coefficients of random variables which need not have normal distributions. This problem is somewhat more involved, although the same approach will be used. To motivate this approach, drop the assumption that the distribution of $W_1$ and $W_2$ is bivariate normal. Assume only that both $\sigma_1$ and $\sigma_2$ are finite and positive. For this case, the expression for $E(W_2|W_1 = w)$ given for the normal case does not hold in general. In fact, $E(W_2|W_1 = w)$ may not even be a linear function of $w$. However, what can be said (e.g., see CRAMÈR 1946, p. 273) is that the expression for the normal case still provides the best linear estimate of $E(W_2|W_1 = w)$ according to the principle of least squares. In other words, the linear function $g(W_1) = \alpha + \beta W_1$ that minimizes $E\{(W_2 - g(W_1))^2\}$ is

$$g(W_1) = E(W_2) - \rho \frac{\sigma_2}{\sigma_1} E(W_1) + \rho \frac{\sigma_2}{\sigma_1} W_1 .$$

Denoting $g(w)$ by $\text{Est}\{E(W_2|W_1 = w)\}$ and rearranging terms,

$$\text{Est}\{E(W_2|W_1 = w)\} = E(W_2) + \rho \frac{\sigma_2}{\sigma_1} (w - E(W_1)) .$$

This function describes what is commonly referred to as the mean square regression line of $W_2$ on $W_1$. Since it would be very difficult to base a subjective estimate of $\rho$ on a non-linear function, this line seems to provide a practical and reasonable basis for the estimation.

By using the mean square regression line, the desired estimate of $\rho$ could be obtained in exactly the manner that was described for the normal case. However, rather than dealing with expected values directly, the simplified estimating process described in Section A.1 may be used instead. To do this, assume that $W_1$ and $W_2$ each have a Beta distribution with six standard deviations lying between the bounds. Additionally, assume that the conditional distribution of $W_2$, given the value taken on by $W_1$, is a Beta distribution with six standard deviations lying between its bounds. Then proceed as follows. Select one or more possible values of $W_1$ other than $E(W_1)$. For each value, estimate the upper bound (optimistic estimate), the lower bound (pessimistic estimate), and mode (most likely estimate) for the conditional distribution of $W_2$. By using the expression given in Section A.1, these three values determine an estimate of the conditional expected value, $\text{Est}\{E(W_2|W_1 = w)\}$. This estimate determines a value for $\rho$ from the equation for the mean square regression line. This value or a suitable weighting of a number of such values is the desired estimate of $\rho$.

Two general questions remain to be answered. First, which values of $W_1$ should be selected for this estimating process? Second, if more than one value of $W_1$ is selected, how should the corresponding estimates of $\rho$ be combined to provide the desired composite estimate?

From the analyst's point of view, the most meaningful values of $W_1$ for this purpose would seem to be its bounds, i.e., the optimistic estimate and pessimistic estimate. It is therefore proposed that these two values be used, which should be sufficient in most cases.

Since the expression for $\text{Est}\{E(W_2|W_1 = w)\}$ was based on the principle of least squares, one might assume that the composite estimate of $\rho$, the slope of the mean square regression line, should be based on this same principle. However, this would only be appropriate if the values of $W_1$ used were random observations from the distribution of $W_1$ rather than arbitrary selections. Therefore, it is suggested that an unweighted average of the two (or more) individual estimates of $\rho$ be used as the desired composite estimate of $\rho$. This procedure is convenient and consistent with the accuracy of the individual estimates.

## A.5. Determination of S

The specification of the set of feasible solutions, $S$, amounts to specifying the various permissible (although not necessarily desirable) combinations of the $m$ proposed investments, and then expressing these combinations in terms of the $\delta$ vectors. Alternatively, it amounts to specifying those combinations which are not permissible, expressing them in terms of the $\delta$ vectors, and then deleting them from the set $\{\delta|\delta_j = 0 \text{ or } 1; \ j = 1, ..., m\}$.

Since the circumstances that dictate the feasibility or lack of feasibility of combinations of investments are often unique to the individual situation, no remarks will be made about the general procedure for determining $S$. However, the reader may refer to WEINGARTNER (1963, Sections 2.3, 3.6, 3.7, 7.1, 7.2, etc.) to see how to express certain common types of capital budgeting restrictions as linear programming constraints.

## A.6. Estimation of competitive or complementary effects

Since there may be as many as $2^m$ distinct feasible $\delta$ vectors, the specification of $h_j(\delta)$, the function describing competitive or complementary effects for period $j$ in the model of Chapter 3, could be a very large task. Fortunately, since only a relatively small number of investments would normally be competitive or complementary, this task can usually be greatly simplified and the number of required estimates greatly reduced. The procedure for achieving this simplification attempts to minimize the amount of analysis required by reducing as much as possible of the task to a routine process that can be performed by a clerk. This procedure will now be presented, followed by a discussion of the required estimates.

The first step is for an analyst to determine which pairs of investments are competitive or complementary. This may be indicated by constructing a table with $m$ rows and $m$ columns (one row and one column for each investment) and inserting a check whenever the investments for that row and that column, respectively, are competitive or complementary. (Since this table or matrix would be symmetrical about its diagonal, only one side of the diagonal would need to be considered.) Alternatively, the analyst may make a list for investment $j$ $(j = 1, 2, ..., m-1)$ of all investments $k$, $k > j$, which are competitive with or complementary to investment $j$.

A more fundamental question is the criterion for deciding when a pair of investments are competitive or complementary. It should be understood that cash flows may be correlated without any competitive or complementary effects being involved. When cash flows from two investments are, for example, positively correlated, the cash flows from one tend to be higher/lower than expected if the cash flows from the other turn out to be higher/lower than expected. This effect is completely distinct from a competitive or complementary effect. The latter effects have to do with the "additivity" of the total cash flows. More precisely, two investments are competitive or complementary if the total expected cash flow from making both investments is not equal to the sum of their expected cash flows if the other investment were not made. Although the use of the mode is not quite equivalent, in general, to the use of the expected value, it should be adequate to ask the analyst to decide if the most likely total cash flow from making both investments is more (complementary effect), less (competitive effect), or the same (no such effects) as the sum of his previous most likely estimates for the investments made individually. This underlying criterion, coupled with a normal interpretation of the terms, competitive and complementary, should enable the analyst to make these decisions.

Given a list of the pairs of investments which are either competitive or complementary, the following routine tasks should be performed. For investment $j$, partition those investments which are competitive with or complementary to investment $j$ into as many lists as possible such that no investment appears on more than one list and competitive or complementary investments appear on the same list. In other words, partition the set of investments which are competitive with or complementary to investment $j$ into as many disjoint subsets as possible such that no investment in one subset is competitive with or complementary to any investment in any other subset. Add investment $j$ to each of these lists (subsets). Perform this process independently for $j = 1, 2, ..., m$. Then combine any lists which have more than one investment in common (and eliminate any list which is a subset of another list). This will insure that any set of mutually competitive or complementary investments appears on exactly one list. Denote the total number of these lists by $L$, the size of the $l$th list by $n_l$, and the index number associated with the $k$th investment of the $l$th list by $s(l, k)$. Next, for each of the $L$ lists, write down all possible combinations of two or more investments on the list. This amounts to listing all vectors of the form $(\delta_{s(l,1)}, \delta_{s(l,2)}, ..., \delta_{s(l,n_l)})$, such that at least two elements equal one and all remaining elements equal zero. Finally, eliminate any combinations which are not feasible, i.e., which are not a subset of any set of investments whose approval would correspond to an element of $S$. Denote the set of all remaining combinations by $R$.

Once $R$ has been obtained, the stage is set for an analyst to resume making judgment decisions. He is required, in brief, to estimate the competitive or complementary effect for each element of $R$ over each of the time periods. He accomplishes this by estimating the expected total cash flow (perhaps by the procedure of Section A.1) if all the investments corresponding to that element of $R$, but no others, were approved. Subtracting the grand sum of the previous estimates for the expected cash flows from each of these investments, if each were the only one approved, gives the desired estimate of the competitive or complementary effect for that element of $R$. Alternatively, he may directly estimate this difference. Although this estimate must be obtained for each time period, $j = 1, 2, \ldots,$ $n$, it is probable that general relationships can be found between periods (such as the effect being a fixed percentage of the grand sum of individual cash flows), so that only minor adjustments should be required after the estimate has been obtained for a typical time period.

For each list $(l = 1, 2, \ldots, L)$ and each time period $(j = 1, 2, \ldots, n)$, define the function $h_j^{(l)}(\delta_{s(l,1)}, \delta_{s(l,2)}, \ldots, \delta_{s(l,n_l)})$ as taking on the value of the estimate of the competitive or complementary effect for the $j$th time period for $(\delta_{s(l,1)}, \delta_{s(l,2)}, \ldots, \delta_{s(l,n_l)})$, if such an estimate is required, and taking on the value zero otherwise. Thus, $h_j^{(l)}$ describes the competitive or complementary effect for the $j$th time period for any subset of the investments on the $l$th list. Since any set of mutually competitive or complementary investments appears on exactly one list,

$$\text{Est}\{h_j(\delta_1, \delta_2, \ldots, \delta_m)\} = \sum_{l=1}^{L} h_j^{(l)}(\delta_{s(l,1)}, \delta_{s(l,2)}, \ldots, \delta_{s(l,n_l)}).$$

## A.7. Estimation of the utility function

Following is a rather brief discussion of how a management group might estimate $U(p)$, their conception of the firm's utility function of total present value, by using the piece-wise quadratic approximation introduced in Section 5.1. The reader is referred to MARKOWITZ (1959, Ch. 10) for more details on the theory and use of utility functions.

Because of the assumptions made about the nature of the $U(p)$ function, the marginal utility function $U'(p)$ is a piece-wise linear function such that $U'(0) = 1$ and $U''(0) = 0$. Therefore, it will prove sufficient to estimate the break points $(p_1, \ldots, p_{M-1})$ in $U'(p)$ and the value of $U'(p)$ at each of these break points in order to completely determine $U'(p)$ and $U(p)$.

For simplicity of presentation, it is assumed that the unit of money is a dollar, although a different denomination would often be used.

An intuitive interpretation of marginal utility is the following. The marginal utility is the rate at which utility increases as the total present value increases. Thus, $U'(p)$ indicates the increase in utility as total present value increases from $p$ to $(p+1)$ [assuming that $U'(p)$ is constant over this region]. Since $U'(0) = 1$, $U'(p)$ represents how much an additional dollar (of total present value) above $p$ would be worth relative to the first dollar. Would one be willing to exert the same amount of effort and take the same risks (no more and no less) in order to try to raise total present value from $p$ to $(p+1)$ as one would be willing to do in order to try to increase it from 0 to 1? If so, $U'(p) = 1$. If not, how much of an increase above $p$ would be equivalent to an increase from 0 to 1? This amount would be $1/U'(p)$.

Another interpretation of marginal utility is that, for any $\varepsilon > 0$, $U(p+\varepsilon) - U(p)$ is just the area under the $U'(\cdot)$ curve from $p$ to $(p+\varepsilon)$. Therefore, if $p$ is positive/negative, $U(p)$ is the positive/negative value of the area under the $U'(\cdot)$ curve from 0 to $p$. One would be indifferent between two alternatives which have the same expected utility.

Now consider how one might estimate the marginal utility at a given point. Let this point be $k_3$, and suppose that there are two other points, $k_1$ and $k_2$ ($k_1 < k_2 < k_3$ or $k_1 > k_2 > k_3$), such that $U'(k_1)$ and $U'(k_2)$ are already known. Assume, in addition, that $U'(p)$ is linear between $k_1$ and $k_2$, and between $k_2$ and $k_3$. $U'(k_3)$ may then be obtained by proceeding as follows. Consider two hypothetical alternatives. One of these is certain to have a total present value equal to $k_2$. The other one will have a total present value of either $k_3$ or $k_1$, where the probabilities are $q$ (i.e., $100q$ chances out of 100) and $1-q$, respectively. Compare these two alternatives and select the value of $q$, denote it as $q^*$, at which one would be completely indifferent between them. It is now known that $(1-q^*)U(k_1) + q^*U(k_3) = U(k_2)$. Therefore, $q^*$ times the area under the $U'(p)$ curve from $k_1$ to $k_3$ must equal the area under the $U'(p)$ curve from $k_1$ to $k_2$. $U'(k_3)$ can now be found by very simple algebra and arithmetic.

A useful corollary to the above result is the following. Assume that $U(p)$ is known for positive values of $p$, and it is desired to find $U(p')$ where $p'$ is negative. Find the smallest positive value of $p$, call it $p^*$, such that one would be willing to risk obtaining a present value of $p'$ in order to have an equal chance of obtaining a present value of $p^*$. The result is that $U(p') = -U(p^*)$. Equivalently, the areas under the $U'(p)$ curve from 0 to

$p^*$ and from 0 to $p'$ would be equal.

A sophisticated analyst might prefer to estimate $p_j$ and $U'(p_j)$, for $j = 1, 2, ..., M-1$, directly. However, for whose who prefer a more straightforward, systematic procedure for estimating $U'(p)$ and $U(p)$, the following approach is suggested. Select a value $K$ for the minimum size of the interval for a linear segment of $U'(p)$. This value should be interpreted as the smallest amount of money (present value) which would have a clearly discernable impact. As will be seen, both the number of estimates required and (up to a point) the accuracy of the estimation of $U(p)$ increase as $K$ is decreased. Therefore, an economic balance is required. Since $U'(0) = 1$, assume that $U'(p) = 1$ for $-K \leqslant p \leqslant K$. Then, beginning with $j = 1$, select the value $q_j^*$ such that one would be completely indifferent between having a total present value equal to $jK$, or having a total present value of either $(j-1)K$ or $(j+1)K$ with associated probabilities of $(1 - q_j^*)$ and $q_j^*$, respectively. Select $q_j^*$ for $j = 1, 2, 3$, etc., in succession until $jK$ is such a large value of total present value as to be outside the realm of reasonable possibility, in which case arbitrarily set $q_j^* = \frac{1}{2}$ (i.e., set $U'(p) = U'(jK)$ for $p \geqslant jK$). Previous discussion has indicated that $U'(p)$ and $U(p)$ can easily be found, for $p \geqslant 0$, from this information. (An alternative approach that would avoid choosing probabilities is to fix $q_j^* = \frac{1}{2}$ for all $j$ and then successively select the corresponding interval sizes instead.) Next, use the procedure outlined in the preceding paragraph to find $U'(p)$ and $U(p)$ for $p < 0$. Thus, beginning with $j = 2$, select the smallest positive value of $p$, call it $p_j^*$, such that one would be willing to risk obtaining a present value of $-jK$ in order to have an equal chance of obtaining a present value of $p$. Select $p_j^*$ for $j = 2, 3, 4$, etc., in succession until $(-jK)$ is such a large negative value of total present value as to be outside the realm of reasonable possibility. Because of the assumption that $U'(p)$ is a piece-wise linear function (and that $U(p) = -p$ for $-K \leqslant p \leqslant 0$), this determines $U'(p)$ and $U(p)$ for $-j^*K \leqslant p \leqslant 0$, where $j^*$ is the largest value of $j$ considered. Assume that $U'(p) = U'(-j^*K)$ for $p \leqslant -j^*K$. $U(p)$ would now be completely specified for all $p$.

It should be emphasized that anyone using this procedure should previously have acquired an understanding of the meaning of present value.

# BIBLIOGRAPHY

ALCHIAN, A. A., "The meaning of utility measurement", *American Economic Review*, Vol. XLIII, No. 1, March, 1953, pp. 26–50.

ANDERSON, T. W., *Introduction to multivariate statistical analysis*, John Wiley and Sons, New York, 1958.

ANGELL, J. W., "Uncertainty, likelihoods and investment decisions", *Quarterly Journal of Economics*, Feb., 1960.

ANSOFF, H. I., "A model for diversification", *Management Science*, July, 1958, pp. 392–414.

APOSTOL, T. M., *Mathematical analysis*, Addison-Wesley, Reading, Mass., 1957.

ARCHIBALD, G. C., "Utility, risk, and linearity", *Journal of Political Economy*, Oct., 1959, pp. 437–439.

ARROW, K. J., "Alternative approaches to the theory of choice in risk taking situations", *Econometrica*, Vol. XIX, No. 1, Oct., 1951a, pp. 404–437.

ARROW, K. J., *Social choice and individual values*, John Wiley and Sons, New York, 1951b.

ARROW, K. J., "Statistics and political economy", *Econometrica*, Oct., 1957.

ARROW, K. J., "Functions of a theory of behavior under uncertainty", *Metroeconomica*, April-August, 1959, pp. 12–20.

ARROW, K. J., "Discounting and public investment criteria", paper given at 1965 Western Resources Conference, July 6, 1965.

BALAS, EGON, "An additive algorithm for solving linear programs with zero–one variables", *Operations Research*, Vol. 13, 1965, pp. 517–546.

BALINSKI, M. L., "Integer programming: methods, uses, computation", *Management Science*, Vol. 12, 1965, pp. 253–313.

BARISH, NORMAN N., *Economic analysis for engineering and managerial decision-making*, McGraw-Hill, New York, 1962.

BAUMOL, W. J., *Economic theory and operations analysis*, Prentice-Hall, Englewood Cliffs, N. J., 1961.

BAUMOL, W. J., "An expected gain-confidence limit criterion for portfolio selection", *Management Science*, Vol. 10, No. 1, Oct., 1963, pp. 174–182.

BAUMOL, W. J., AND QUANDT, R. E., "Mathematical programming and the discount rate under capital rationing", *Economic Journal*, June, 1965, pp. 317–329.

BEALE, E. M. L., "Survey of integer programming", *Operational Research Quarterly*, Vol. 16, 1965, pp. 219–228.

BERNHARD, RICHARD H., "Discount methods for expenditure evaluation–A clarification of their assumptions", *The Journal of Industrial Engineering*, Jan.–Feb., 1962, pp. 19–27.

BIERMAN, HAROLD, JR., *Topics in cost accounting and decisions*, McGraw-Hill, New York, 1963.

BIERMAN, HAROLD, JR., AND SMIDT, SEYMOUR, "Capital budgeting and the problem of reinvesting cash proceeds", *Journal of Business*, Oct., 1957.

BIERMAN, HAROLD, JR., AND SMIDT, SEYMOUR, *The capital budgeting decision*, The MacMillan Company, New York, 1960.

BIRKHOFF, G., AND MACLANE, S., *A survey of modern algebra*, The MacMillan Company, New York, 1948.

BODENHORN, DIRAN, "On the problem of capital budgeting", *The Journal of Finance*, Vol. XIV, Dec., 1959, pp. 473–492.

BOOT, J. C. G., AND THEIL, H., "A procedure for integer maximization of a definite quadratic function", Reprint Series No. 93 (Econometric Institute of the Netherlands School of Economics), Publication No. 23 of the International Center for Management Science, Rotterdam. First issued in 1963.

BORCH, KARL, "A note on utility and attitudes to risk", *Management Science*, Vol. 9, No. 4, July, 1963, pp. 697–700.

BORCH, KARL, "A utility function derived from survival games", *Management Science*, Vol. 12, No. 8, April, 1966, pp. B-287 to B-295.

BOULDING, KENNETH, "General systems theory–a skeleton of science", *Management Science*, April, 1956, pp. 197–208.

BOWKER, ALBERT H., AND LIEBERMAN, GERALD J., *Engineering statistics*, Prentice-Hall, Englewood Cliffs, N.J., 1959.

BOWMAN, M. J., ed., *Expectations, uncertainty and business behavior*, New York, 1958.

CANDLER, WILFRED, AND TOWNSLEY, ROBERT J., "The maximization of a quadratic function of variables subject to linear inequalities", *Management Science*, Vol. 10, No. 3, April, 1964, pp. 515–523.

CARTER, C. F., MEREDITY, G. P., AND SCHACKLE, G. L. S., *Uncertainty and business decisions*, Liverpool University Press, 1957.

CHAMBERS, D., AND CHARNES, A., "Inter-temporal analysis and optimization of bank portfolios", *Management Science*, July, 1961, pp. 393–410.

CHARNES, A., AND COOPER, W. W., "Chance-constrained programming", *Management Science*, Oct., 1959a, pp. 73–79.

CHARNES, A., AND COOPER, W. W., "Chance-constrained programs with normal deviates and linear decision rules", The Technological Institute, Northwestern University, 1959b.

CHARNES, A., AND COOPER, W. W., *Management models and industrial applications of linear programming*, I, II, John Wiley and Sons, New York, 1961.

CHARNES, A., AND COOPER, W. W., "Systems evaluations and repricing theorems", *Management Science*, Oct., 1962a, pp. 33–49.

CHARNES, A., AND COOPER, W. W., "Chance constraints and normal deviates", *Journal of the American Statistical Association*, March, 1962b, pp. 134–143.

CHARNES, A., AND COOPER, W. W., "Deterministic equivalents for optimizing and satisfying under chance constraints", *Operations Research*, Vol. 11, 1963, pp. 18–39.

CHARNES, A., COOPER, W. W., AND MELLON, BOB, "A model for programming and sensitivity analysis in an integrated oil company", *Econometrica*, 1954, pp. 193–217.

CHARNES, A., COOPER, W. W., AND MILLER, M. H., "Application of linear programming to financial budgeting and the costing of funds", *Journal of Business*, Jan., 1959.

CHARNES, A., COOPER, W. W., AND SYMONDS, G. H., "Cost horizons and certainty equivalents: An approach to stochastic programming of heating oil", *Management Science*, April, 1958, pp. 235–263.

CHENG, PAO-LUN, "Optimum bond portfolio selection", *Management Science*, July, 1962, pp. 490–499.

COHEN, KALMAN J., AND FITCH, BRUCE P., "The average investment performance index", *Management Science*, Vol. 12, No. 6, Feb., 1966, pp. B-195 to B-215.

COOMBS, C. H., AND PRUITT, D. G., "Components of risk in decision making: probability and variance preferences", *Journal of Experimental Psychology*, Nov., 1960.

CORD, JOEL, "A method for allocating funds to investment projects when returns are subject to uncertainty", *Management Science*, Jan., 1964.

CRAMÈR, HARALD, *Mathematical methods of statistics*, Princeton University Press, Princeton, 1946.

CYERT, R. M., and MARCH, J. G., "The role of expectations in business decision making", *Administrative Science Quarterly*, Dec., 1958.

CYERT, R. M., AND MARCH, J. G., "Introduction to a behavioral theory of organizational objectives", in *Modern organization theory*, edited by M. Haire, John Wiley and Sons, New York, 1959.

DANTZIG, GEORGE B., "Linear programming under uncertainty", *Management Science*, Vol. 1, 1955, pp. 197–206.

DEAN, JOEL, *Capital budgeting*, Columbia University Press, New York, 1951.

DEAN, JOEL, "Measuring the productivity of capital", *Harvard Business Review*, Vol. 32, Jan.–Feb., 1954, pp. 120–130.

DEGARMO, E. PAUL, *Engineering economy*, 3rd edition, The MacMillan Company, New York, 1960.

DOOB, J. L., *Stochastic processes*, John Wiley and Sons, New York, 1953.

DORFMAN, ROBERT, SAMUELSON, PAUL A., AND SOLOW, ROBERT, *Linear programming and economic analysis*, McGraw-Hill, New York, 1958, Appendix A.

DUNCAN, D. C., "The concept of potential surprise", *Metroeconomica*, April–August, 1959, pp. 21–36.

DURAND, DAVID, "Costs of debt and equity funds for business: trends and problems of measurements", Conference on Research in Business Finance, pp. 215–247. National Bureau of Economic Research, New York, 1952.

DURAND, DAVID, "The cost of capital, corporation finance and the theory of investment: comment", *American Economic Review*, Vol. XLIX, Sept., 1959, pp. 639–655.

DYCKMAN, T. R., "Allocating funds to investment projects when funds are subject to uncertainty: a comment", *Management Science*, Vol. 11, No. 2, Nov., 1964, pp. 348–350.

EDWARDS, WARD, "The theory of decision making", *Psychological Bulletin*, July, 1954.

EGERTON, R. A., *Investment decisions under uncertainty*, Liverpool University Press, 1960.

EGGLESTON, H. G., *Convexity*, Cambridge University Press, Cambridge, England, 1958.

ENGLISH, J. MORLEY, "New approaches to economic comparison for engineering projects", *The Journal of Industrial Engineering*, Nov.–Dec., 1961, pp. 375–378.

FAMA, EUGENE F., "Portfolio analysis in a stable paretian market", *Management Science*, Vol. 11, No. 3, Jan., 1965, pp. 404–419.

FARRAR, DONALD EUGENE, *The investment decision under uncertainty*, Prentice-Hall, Englewood Cliffs, N.J., 1962.

FELLER, WILLIAM, *An introduction to probability theory and its applications*, 2nd edition, John Wiley and Sons, New York, 1957.

FISHER, I., "A statistical method for measuring marginal utility", in *Economic essays in honor of J. B. Clark*, edited by J. H. Hollander, The MacMillan Company,

New York, 1927.

FISHER, I., *The theory of interest*, The MacMillan Company, New York, 1930; reprinted, Kelly and Millman, New York, 1954.

FOLDES, L. E., "Uncertainty, probability, and potential surprise", *Economica*, August, 1958, pp. 246–254.

FRASER, D. A. S., *Non-parametric methods in statistics*, John Wiley and Sons, New York, 1957.

FREUND, R. J., "The introduction of risk into a programming model", *Econometrica*, July, 1961.

FRIEDMAN, MILTON, AND SAVAGE, L. J., "The utility analysis of choices involving risk", *Journal of Political Economy*, Vol. LVI, No. 4, August, 1948, pp. 279-304.

GAVER, D. P., JR., "Models for appraising investments yielding stochastic returns", *Management Science*, Vol. 11, No. 9, July, 1965, pp. 815–830.

GLOVER, FRED, "A multiphase-dual algorithm for the zero–one integer programming problem", *Operations Research*, Vol. 13, No. 6, Nov.–Dec., 1965, pp. 879–919.

GNEDENKO, B. V., "Limit theorems of probability theory", *Proceedings of the International Congress of Mathematicians*, 1958.

GOMORY, R. E., "Outline of an algorithm for integer solutions to linear programs", *Bulletin of the American Mathematical Society*, Sept., 1958a, pp. 275–278.

GOMORY, R. E., "An algorithm for integer solutions to linear programs", *Princeton-IBM Mathematics Research Project Technical Report*, No. 1, Princeton, N. J., Nov., 1958b.

GOMORY, R. E., "All-integer integer programming algorithm", *IBM Research Report*, RC-189, Yorktown Heights, Jan., 1960.

GOMORY, R. E., AND BAUMOL, W. H., "Integer programming and pricing", *Econometrica*, July, 1960, pp. 521–550.

GORDON, MYRON J., AND SHAPIRO, ELI, "Capital equipment analysis: the required rate of profit", *Management Science*, Oct., 1956, pp. 102–110.

GORDON, MYRON J., *The investment, financing, and valuation of the corporation*, Richard D. Irwin, Homewood, Ill., 1962.

GORMAN, W. M., "A revised theory of expectations", *Economic Journal*, Sept., 1957, pp. 549–551.

Grant, EUGENE L., *Statistical quality control*, 2nd edition, McGraw-Hill, New York, 1952.

GRANT, EUGENE L., AND IRESON, W. GRANT, *Principles of engineering economy*, 4th edition, The Ronald Press, New York, 1960.

GREEN, PAUL E., "The derivation of utility functions in a large industrial firm", paper given at the First Joint National Meeting of the Operations Research

Society of America and the Institute of Management Sciences, 1961.

HAAVELMO, TRYGVE, *A study in the theory of investment*, University of Chicago Press, Chicago, 1960.

HALL, ARTHUR D., *A methodology for systems engineering*, D. Van Nostrand, Princeton, N. J., 1962.

HARING, J. E., AND SMITH, G. C., "Utility theory and profit maximization", *American Economic Review*, Sept., 1959.

Hart, A. G., "Anticipations, uncertainty and dynamic planning", *Studies in Business Administration*, XI, No. 1, University of Chicago Press, Chicago, 1940.

HATRY, HARRY P., "Economic analysis as an aid to system selection", *The Journal of Industrial Engineering*, July-August, 1962, pp. 207–212.

HERSTEIN, I. N., AND MILNOR, JOHN, "An axiomatic approach to measurable utility", *Econometrica*, Vol. XXI, No. 2, April, 1953; reprinted as *Cowles Commission Papers, New Series, No. 65*.

HERTZ, D. B., "Risk analysis in capital investment", *Harvard Business Review*, Jan.–Feb., 1964, pp. 95–106.

HESPOS, RICHARD F., AND STRASSMANN, PAUL A., "Stochastic decision trees for the analysis of investment decisions", *Management Science*, Vol. 11, No. 10, August, 1965, pp. B-244 to B-259.

HILL, HORACE, "Capital expenditure management", *Journal of Business*, Oct., 1955.

HILLIER, FREDERICK S., "Derivation of probabilistic information for the evaluation of risky investments", *Management Science*, April, 1963, pp. 443–457.

HILLIER, FREDERICK S., "Supplement to the derivation of probabilistic information for the evaluation of risky investments", *Management Science*, Vol. 11, No. 3, Jan., 1965, pp. 485–487.

HILLIER, FREDERICK S., AND HEEBINK, DAVID V., "Evaluating risky capital investments", *California Management Review*, Winter, 1965–1966, pp. 71–80.

HILLIER, FREDERICK S., "Efficient suboptimal algorithms for integer linear programming with an interior", *Technical Report No. 2*, Contract Nonr-225(89), Stanford University, Aug. 12, 1966a. Submitted to *Operations Research*.

HILLIER, FREDERICK S., "An optimal bound-and-scan algorithm for integer linear programming", *Technical Report No. 3*, Contract Nonr-225(89), Stanford University, August 19, 1966b. Submitted to *Operations Research*.

HILLIER, FREDERICK S., "Chance-constrained programming with 0–1 or bounded continuous decision variables", *Management Science*, Vol. 14, No. 1, Sept., 1967a, pp. 34–51.

HILLIER, FREDERICK S., AND LIEBERMAN, GERALD J., *Introduction to operations research*, Holden-Day, San Francisco, 1967b.

HIRSCHLEIFER, J., "On the theory of optimal investment decision", *Journal of*

*Political Economy*, August, 1958, pp. 329–352.

HIRSCHLEIFER, J., "Efficient allocation of capital in an uncertain world", *American Economic Review*, May, 1964, pp. 77–85.

HOEFFDING, W., AND ROBBINS, H., "The central limit theorem for dependent random variables", *Duke Mathematical Journal*, Vol. 15, 1948, pp. 773 ff.

HOROWITZ, IRA, "The plant investment decision revisited", *Journal of Industrial Engineering*, Vol. XVII, No. 8, August, 1966, pp. 416–422.

ISTVAN, DONALD F., "The economic evaluation of capital expenditures", *Journal of Business*, Vol. XXXIV, No. 1, Jan., 1961.

KALECKI, M., "The principle of increasing risk", *Economica*, Vol. 4, Nov., 1937, pp. 440–447.

KALECKI, M., "A comment on the principle of increasing risk; a reply", *Economica*, Vol. 5, Nov., 1938, pp. 459–460.

KATAOKA, SHINJI, "A stochastic programming model", *Econometrica*, Vol. 31, 1963, pp. 181–196.

KAUFMAN, GORDON M., "Sequential investment analysis under uncertainty", *Journal of Business*, Vol. XXXVI, No. 1, Jan., 1963, pp. 39–64.

KNIGHT, FRANK, *Risk, uncertainty, and profit*, Houghton-Mifflin Co., Boston, 1921.

KUH, EDWIN, "Capital theory and capital budgeting", *Metroeconomica*, Vol. XII, August-Dec., 1960, pp. 64–80.

KUNZI, HANS P., AND OETTLI, WERNER, "Integer quadratic programming", *Recent advances in mathematical programming*, edited by R. L. Graves and P. Wolfe, McGraw-Hill, New York, 1963, pp. 303–308.

LATANÉ, H. A., "Criteria for choice among risky ventures", *Journal of Political Economy*, April, 1959.

LITTLE, JOHN D., MURTY, KATTA G., SWEENEY, DURA W., AND CAROLINE, KAREL, "An algorithm for the traveling salesman problem", *Operations research*, Vol. 11, 1963, pp. 972–989.

LOÉVE, MICHEL, *Probability theory*, 2nd edition, D. Van Nostrand, Princeton, N.J., 1960.

LORIE, J., AND SAVAGE, L. J., "Three problems in capital rationing", *Journal of Business*, Oct., 1955.

LUCE, R. DUNCAN, AND RAIFFA, HOWARD, *Games and decisions; introduction and critical survey*, John Wiley and Sons, New York, 1957.

LUTZ, FREDERICK AND LUTZ, VERA, *The theory of investment of the firm*, Princeton University Press, Princeton, N.J., 1951.

MAGEE, JOHN F., "Decision trees for decision making", *Harvard Business Review*, July–August, 1964a.

MAGEE, JOHN F., "How to use decision trees in capital investment", *Harvard*

*Business Review*, Sept.–Oct., 1964b.

MALCOLM, D. G., ROSEBOOM, J. H., AND CLARK, C. E., "Application of a technique for research and development program evaluation", *Operations Research*, Sept.–Oct., 1959, pp. 646–669.

MAO, JAMES C. T., AND SÄRNDAL, CARL ERIK, "A decision theory approach to portfolio selection", *Management Science*, Vol. 12, No. 8, April, 1966, pp. B-323 to B-333.

MARGLIN, S., *Approaches to dynamic investment planning*, North-Holland Publishing Company, Amsterdam, 1963.

MARKOWITZ, HARRY M., "The utility of wealth", *Journal of Political Economy*, Vol. LX, No. 2, April, 1952, pp. 151–158.

MARKOWITZ, HARRY M., *Portfolio selection*, John Wiley and Sons, New York, 1959.

MARSCHAK, JACOB, "Rational behavior, uncertain prospects, and measurable utility", Econometrica, Vol. XVIII, No. 2, April, 1950; reprinted as *Cowles Commission Papers, New Series, No. 43*.

MARTIN, A. D., JR., "Mathematical programming of portfolio selections", *Management Science*, Jan., 1954, pp. 152–165.

MASON, THOMAS E., AND HAZARD, CLIFTON T., *Brief analytic geometry*, 2nd edition, Ginn and Company, Boston, 1947.

MASSÉ, PIERRE, *Optimal investment decisions*, Prentice-Hall, Englewood Cliffs, N.J., 1962.

MILLER, MERTON H., AND MODIGLIANI, FRANCO, "Dividend policy, growth, and the valuation of shares", *Journal of Business*, Vol. XXXIV, No. 4, Oct., 1961, pp. 411–433.

MODIGLIANI, F., AND BRUMBERG, R., "Utility analysis and the consumption", *Post Kensian Economics*, edited by K. Kurihara, Rutgers University Press, 1954.

MODIGLIANI, F., AND COHEN, K. J., "The role of anticipations and plans in economic behavior and their use in economic analysis and forecasting", *Studies in business expectations and planning*, No. 4, Bureau of Economic and Business Research, University of Illinois, Urbana, Ill., 1961.

MODIGLIANI, F., AND MILLER, M., "The cost of capital, corporation finance, and the theory of investment", *American Economic Review*, Vol. XLVIII, No. 2, June, 1958.

MODIGLIANI, F., AND MILLER, M., "The cost of capital, corporation finance, and theory of investment; reply", *American Economic Review*, Vol. XLIX, Sept., 1959, pp. 655–669.

MOOD, ALEXANDER, *Introduction to the theory of statistics*, McGraw-Hill, New York, 1950.

MORRIS, WILLIAM T., "Diversification", *Management Science*, July, 1958, pp.

381–391.

MORRIS, WILLIAM T., *Engineering economy*, Richard D. Irwin, Homewood, Ill., 1960.

MOSTELLER, C. F., AND NOGEE, P., "An experimental measure of utility", *Journal of Political Economy*, Oct., 1951.

NASLUND, BERTIL, "Mathematical programming under risk", *Swedish Journal of Economics*, 1965, pp. 240–255.

NASLUND, BERTIL, "A model of capital budgeting under risk", *Journal of Business*, Vol. XXXIX, 1966, pp. 257–271.

NASLUND, BERTIL, AND WHINSTON, ANDREW, "A model of multi-period investment under uncertainty", *Management Science*, Jan., 1962, pp. 184–200.

PRATT, J. W., "Risk aversion in the small and in the large", *Econometrica*, Jan.–April, 1964a, pp. 122–136.

PRATT, J. W., RAIFFA, HOWARD, AND SCHLAIFER, ROBERT, "The foundations of decision under uncertainty: An elementary exposition", *Journal of the American Statistical Association*, Vol. 59, June, 1964b, pp. 353–375.

REISMAN, ARNOLD, AND BUFFA, ELWOOD S., "A general model for investment policy", *Management Science*, April, 1962, pp. 304–310.

REITER, STANLEY, "Choosing an investment program among interdependent projects", *Review of Economic Studies*, Jan., 1963, pp. 32–36.

REITER, STANLEY, AND RICE, DONALD B., "Discrete optimizing solution procedures for linear and nonlinear integer programming problems", Institute Paper No. 109, Institute for Research in the Behavioral, Economic, and Management Sciences, Purdue University, Lafayette, Indiana, May, 1965.

RENSHAW, E., "A note on the arithmetic of capital budgeting decisions", *Journal of Business*, July, 1957.

ROBERTS, H. V., "Current problems in the economics of capital budgeting", *Journal of Business*, Jan., 1957.

ROBICHEK, A. A., TEICHROEW, D., AND JONES, J. M., "Optimal short-term financing decision", *Management Science*, Vol. 12, No. 1, Sept., 1965, pp. 1–36.

SAVAGE, LEONARD J., *The foundations of statistics*, John Wiley and Sons, New York, 1954.

SCHLAIFER, ROBERT, *Probability and statistics for business decisions*, McGraw-Hill, New York, 1959.

SHACKLE, G. L. S., *Uncertainty in economics and other reflections*, Cambridge University Press, 1955.

SHACKLE, G. L. S., *Decisions, order and time in human affairs*, Cambridge University Press 1961.

SHARPE, WILLIAM, F., "A simplified model for portfolio analysis", *Management*

*Science*, Jan., 1963, pp. 277–292.

SIMON, HERBERT, *Models of man*, John Wiley and Sons, New York, 1957.

SIMON, HERBERT, "Theories of decision making in economics", *American Economic Review*, June, 1959.

SOLOMON, EZRA, *The theory of financial management*, Columbia University Press, New York and London, 1953.

SOLOMON, EZRA, "Measuring a company's cost of capital", *Journal of Business*, Oct., 1955.

SOLOMON, EZRA, ed., *The management of corporate capital*, a publication of the Graduate School of Business, The University of Chicago, Third Series, published by the Free Press of Glencoe, Illinois, 1959.

SOLOMON, MARTIN B., JR., "Uncertainty and its effect on capital investment analysis", *Management Science*, Vol. 12, No. 8, April, 1966, pp. B-334 to B-339.

SOULE, R. P., "Trends in the cost of capital", *Harvard Business Review*, March–April, 1953, pp. 33–47.

TEICHROEW, DANIEL, ROBICHEK, ALEXANDER A., AND MONTALBANO, MICHAEL, "An analysis of criteria for investment and financing decisions under certainty", *Management Science*, Vol. 12, No. 3, Nov., 1965a, pp. 151–179.

TEICHROEW, DANIEL, ROBICHEK, ALEXANDER A., AND MONTALBANO, MICHAEL, "Mathematical analysis of rates of return under certainty", *Management Science*, Vol. 11, No. 3, Jan., 1965b, pp. 395–403.

VON NEUMANN, JOHN, AND MORGENSTERN, OSKAR, *Theory of games and economic behavior*, 3rd edition, Princeton University Press, Princeton, N.J., 1953.

WEINGARTNER, H. MARTIN, *Mathematical programming and the analysis of capital budgeting problems*, Prentice-Hall, Englewood Cliffs, N.J., 1963.

WEINGARTNER, H. MARTIN, "Capital budgeting of interrelated projects: survey and synthesis", *Management Science*, Vol. 12, No. 7, March, 1966, pp. 485–516.

WILLIAMS, J. B., *The theory of investment value*, Harvard University Press, Cambridge, Mass., 1938.

WOLD, A., MANNE, A. S., SAMUELSON, P. A., MALINVAUD, E., SAVAGE, L. J., AND SHACKLE, G. L. S., "Several related notes on the strong independence axiom of utility theory", *Econometrica*, Vol. XX, No. 4, Oct., 1952, pp. 661–679.

WOLFE, Philip, "The simplex method for quadratic programming", *Econometrica*, July, 1959, pp. 382–398.

WRAY, M. J., "Uncertainty, prices and entrepreneurial expectations", *Journal of Industrial Economics*, Feb., 1956, pp. 107–128.

ZELLNER, ARNOLD, AND CHETTY, V. KARUPPAN, "Prediction and decision problems in regression models from the Bayesian point of view", *Journal of the American Statistical Association*, Vol. 60, June, 1965, pp. 608–616.

# INDEX

111